DEFENSE, SECURITY AND STRATEGIES

NAVY SHIPBOARD LASERS: THE WEAPONS OF TOMORROW

DEFENSE, SECURITY AND STRATEGIES

Additional books in this series can be found on Nova's website under the Series tab.

Additional E-books in this series can be found on Nova's website under the E-books tab.

LASERS AND ELECTRO-OPTICS RESEARCH AND TECHNOLOGY

Additional books in this series can be found on Nova's website under the Series tab.

Additional E-books in this series can be found on Nova's website under the E-books tab.

DEFENSE, SECURITY AND STRATEGIES

NAVY SHIPBOARD LASERS: THE WEAPONS OF TOMORROW

RICHARD E. GRIFFITH
AND
GILLIAN L. COUGHLIN
EDITORS

Nova Science Publishers, Inc.
New York

Copyright © 2011 by Nova Science Publishers, Inc.

All rights reserved. No part of this book may be reproduced, stored in a retrieval system or transmitted in any form or by any means: electronic, electrostatic, magnetic, tape, mechanical photocopying, recording or otherwise without the written permission of the Publisher.

For permission to use material from this book please contact us:
Telephone 631-231-7269; Fax 631-231-8175
Web Site: http://www.novapublishers.com

NOTICE TO THE READER

The Publisher has taken reasonable care in the preparation of this book, but makes no expressed or implied warranty of any kind and assumes no responsibility for any errors or omissions. No liability is assumed for incidental or consequential damages in connection with or arising out of information contained in this book. The Publisher shall not be liable for any special, consequential, or exemplary damages resulting, in whole or in part, from the readers' use of, or reliance upon, this material. Any parts of this book based on government reports are so indicated and copyright is claimed for those parts to the extent applicable to compilations of such works.

Independent verification should be sought for any data, advice or recommendations contained in this book. In addition, no responsibility is assumed by the publisher for any injury and/or damage to persons or property arising from any methods, products, instructions, ideas or otherwise contained in this publication.

This publication is designed to provide accurate and authoritative information with regard to the subject matter covered herein. It is sold with the clear understanding that the Publisher is not engaged in rendering legal or any other professional services. If legal or any other expert assistance is required, the services of a competent person should be sought. FROM A DECLARATION OF PARTICIPANTS JOINTLY ADOPTED BY A COMMITTEE OF THE AMERICAN BAR ASSOCIATION AND A COMMITTEE OF PUBLISHERS.

Additional color graphics may be available in the e-book version of this book.

Library of Congress Cataloging-in-Publication Data

Navy shipboard lasers : the weapons of tomorrow / editors, Richard E. Griffith and Gillian L. Coughlin.
  p. cm.
  Includes bibliographical references and index.
  ISBN 978-1-61324-212-4 (softcover : alk. paper) 1. Laser weapons. 2. Lasers--Military applications. 3. United States. Navy--Weapons systems. I. Griffith, Richard E. II. Coughlin, Gillian L.
  UG486.N38 2011
  623.4'46--dc22
                    2011009071

Published by Nova Science Publishers, Inc. † New York

CONTENTS

Preface		**vii**
Chapter 1	Navy Shipboard Lasers for Surface, Air, and Missile Defense: Background and Issues for Congress *Ronald O'Rourke*	**1**
Chapter 2	Solid-State Fiber Laser *Office of Navy Research*	**61**
Chapter 3	High-Power Fiber Lasers for Directed-Energy Applications *P. Sprangle, A. Ting, J. Peñano, R. Fischer and B. Hafizi*	**65**
Chapter 4	CCW: Article by Article Analysis of the Protocol on Blinding Laser Weapons	**87**
Chapter Sources		**91**
Index		**93**

PREFACE

The Department of Defense's (DOD) development work on high-energy military lasers, which has been underway for decades, has reached the point where lasers capable of countering certain surface and air targets at ranges of about a mile could be made ready for installation on Navy surface ships over the next few years. More powerful shipboard lasers, which could become ready for installation in subsequent years, could provide Navy surface ships with an ability to counter a wider range of surface and air targets at ranges of up to about 10 miles. This book examines Navy shipboard laser technologies and applications for surface, air and missile defense

Chapter 1- Department of Defense (DOD) development work on high-energy military lasers, which has been underway for decades, has reached the point where lasers capable of countering certain surface and air targets at ranges of about a mile could be made ready for installation on Navy surface ships over the next few years. More powerful shipboard lasers, which could become ready for installation in subsequent years, could provide Navy surface ships with an ability to counter a wider range of surface and air targets at ranges of up to about 10 miles. These more powerful lasers might, among other things, provide Navy surface ships with a terminal-defense capability against certain ballistic missiles, including the anti-ship ballistic missile (ASBM) that China is believed to be developing.

Chapter 2- Solid-State Fiber Laser provides Incoherent Fiber Lasers for short asymmetric threat engagement and Coherent Combined Fiber Lasers for long range aircraft self protection.

Chapter 3- High-power fiber lasers can be incoherently combined to form the basis of a high-energy laser system for directed-energy applications. These applications include tactical directed energy and power beaming. Incoherent combining of fiber lasers has a number of advantages over other laser beam combining methods. The incoherently combined laser system is relatively simple, highly efficient, compact, robust, low-maintenance, and reliable. In this article, we characterize the atmospheric propagation of incoherently combined, high optical quality laser beams and compare them with other types of laser beams and combining methods. For tactical directed-energy applications, we find that the propagation efficiency of incoherently combined high optical quality beams is near the theoretical upper limit for any laser system with the same beam director and total power. We present results of the first atmospheric propagation experiments using incoherently combined, kilowatt-class, single-mode fiber lasers. These NRL field experiments combined four fiber lasers using a beam director consisting of individually controlled steering mirrors. The transmitted continuous-wave power was 3 kW at a range of 1.2 km with a demonstrated propagation efficiency of ~90% in moderate atmospheric turbulence. The experimental results are found to be in good agreement with simulations and theory.

Chapter 4- The Protocol on Blinding Laser Weapons (Protocol IV) is annexed to the Convention on Prohibitions or Restriction on the Use of Certain Conventional Weapons Which May be Deemed to be Excessively Injurious or to Have Indiscriminate Effects (the Convention).

The Convention, including three annexed protocols, was concluded at Geneva on October 10, 1980. The United States ratified the Convention and expressed its consent to be bound by its Protocol II on Mines, Booby-traps and Other Devices, as well as its Protocol I on Non-Detectable Fragments, on March 24, 1995.

In: Navy Shipboard Lasers
Editors: R. E. Griffith, G. L. Coughlin

ISBN: 978-1-61324-212-4
© 2011 Nova Science Publishers, Inc.

Chapter 1

NAVY SHIPBOARD LASERS FOR SURFACE, AIR, AND MISSILE DEFENSE: BACKGROUND AND ISSUES FOR CONGRESS[*]

Ronald O'Rourke

SUMMARY

Department of Defense (DOD) development work on high-energy military lasers, which has been underway for decades, has reached the point where lasers capable of countering certain surface and air targets at ranges of about a mile could be made ready for installation on Navy surface ships over the next few years. More powerful shipboard lasers, which could become ready for installation in subsequent years, could provide Navy surface ships with an ability to counter a wider range of surface and air targets at ranges of up to about 10 miles. These more powerful lasers might, among other things, provide Navy surface ships with a terminal-defense capability against certain ballistic missiles, including the anti-ship ballistic missile (ASBM) that China is believed to be developing.

The Navy and DOD are developing three principal types of lasers for potential use on Navy surface ships—fiber solid state lasers (SSLs), slab SSLs, and free electron lasers (FELs). The Navy's fiber SSL prototype

---

[*] This is an edited, reformatted and augmented version of a Congressional Research Services publication, dated January 14, 2011.

demonstrator is called the Laser Weapon System (LaWS). Among DOD's multiple efforts to develop slab SSLs for military use is the Maritime Laser Demonstration (MLD), a prototype laser weapon developed as a rapid demonstration project. The Navy has developed a lower-power FEL prototype and is now developing a prototype with scaled-up power. These lasers differ in terms of their relative merits as potential shipboard weapons.

Although the Navy is developing laser technologies and prototypes of potential shipboard lasers, and has a generalized vision for shipboard lasers, the Navy currently does not have a program of record for procuring a production version of a shipboard laser, or a roadmap that calls for installing lasers on specific surface ships by specific dates. The possibility of equipping Navy surface ships with lasers in coming years raises a number of potential issues for Congress, including the following:

- whether the Navy should act now to adopt a program of record for procuring a production version of a shipboard laser, and/or a roadmap that calls for installing lasers on specific surface ships by specific dates;
- how many types of lasers to continue developing, particularly given constraints on Navy funding, and the relative merits of types currently being developed; and
- the potential implications of shipboard lasers for the design and acquisition of Navy ships, including the Flight III DDG-51 destroyer that the Navy wants to begin procuring in FY2016.

Congress in past years has provided some additional funding to help support Navy development of potential shipboard lasers. For FY2012 and subsequent years, Congress has several options regarding potential shipboard lasers. In addition to decisions on whether or not to fund continued development of potential shipboard lasers, these options include, among other things, the following: encouraging or directing the Navy or some other DOD organization to perform an analysis of alternatives (AOA) comparing the cost-effectiveness of lasers and traditional kinetic weapons (such as missiles and guns) for countering surface, air, and missile targets, and encouraging or directing the Navy to adopt a program of record for procuring a production version of a shipboard laser, and/or a roadmap that calls for installing lasers on specific surface ships by specific dates.

INTRODUCTION

Issue for Congress

Department of Defense (DOD) development work on high-energy military lasers, which has been underway for decades, has reached the point where lasers capable of countering certain surface and air targets at ranges of about a mile could be made ready for installation on Navy surface ships over the next few years. More powerful shipboard lasers, which could become ready for installation in subsequent years, could provide Navy surface ships with an ability to counter a wider range of surface and air targets at ranges of up to about 10 miles. These more powerful lasers might, among other things, provide Navy surface ships with a terminal-defense capability against certain ballistic missiles, including the anti-ship ballistic missile (ASBM) that China is believed to be developing.[1] An August 2010 press report states:

> Experts believe that of all the services the Navy holds the most promise for helping directed energy weapons become operationally viable systems in the near future.... This fall, the Office of Naval Research plans to demonstrate a high-energy laser weapon system prototype at sea for the first time.[2] If that demonstration proves successful at destroying a high-speed boat target, then Navy officials could decide to procure a system and become the first service to incorporate high-powered lasers into its weapon inventory.[3]

Compared to existing ship self-defense systems, such as missiles and guns, lasers could provide Navy surface ships with a more cost effective means of countering certain surface, air, and ballistic missile targets. Ships equipped with a combination of lasers and existing self-defense systems might be able to defend themselves more effectively against a range of such targets. Equipping Navy surface ships with lasers could lead to changes in naval tactics, ship design, and procurement plans for ship-based weapons, bringing about a technological shift for the Navy—a "game changer"—comparable to the advent of shipboard missiles in the 1950s.

Although the Navy is developing laser technologies and prototypes of potential shipboard lasers, and has a generalized vision for shipboard lasers, the Navy currently does not have a program of record[4] for procuring a production version of a shipboard laser, or a roadmap that calls for installing lasers on specific surface ships by specific dates.

The central issue for Congress is whether to approve or modify the Administration's proposed funding levels for development of potential shipboard lasers, and whether to provide the Navy or DOD with direction concerning development and procurement programs for shipboard lasers. Potential specific issues for Congress include the following:

- whether the Navy should act now to adopt a program of record for procuring a production version of a shipboard laser, and/or a roadmap that calls for installing lasers on specific surface ships by specific dates;
- how many types of lasers to continue developing, particularly given constraints on Navy funding, and the relative merits of types currently being developed; and
- the potential implications of shipboard lasers for the design and acquisition of Navy ships, including the Flight III DDG-51 destroyer that the Navy wants to begin procuring in FY2016.

Decisions that Congress makes regarding potential shipboard lasers could significantly affect future Navy capabilities and funding requirements, the U.S. industrial base for military lasers, and the industrial base for existing shipboard self-defense systems.

Scope, Sources, and Terminology

This report focuses on potential Navy shipboard lasers for countering surface, air, and ballistic missile threats. It does not discuss the use of lasers on Navy aircraft or submarines, or the use of lasers by other military services.

This report is based on unclassified information from Navy, RAND,[5] and industry briefings on shipboard lasers provided to CRS and the Congressional Budget Office (CBO) in the summer of 2010, as well as unclassified open-domain information. CRS requested the Navy and industry briefings to support the preparation of this report. Unless otherwise indicated, information presented in this report (including the appendices) is taken from the briefings.

For purposes of this report, the term "short range" generally refers to ranges of one or two nautical miles, while references to longer ranges or extended ranges refer to ranges of up to about 10 nautical miles.[6] Lasers are one type of directed energy weapon (DEW); other DEWs include microwave weapons and millimeter wave weapons.

BACKGROUND

Shipboard Lasers in General

Potential Advantages and Limitations of Shipboard Lasers

Lasers are of interest to the Navy and other observers as potential shipboard weapons because they have certain potential advantages for countering some types of surface, air, and ballistic missile targets. Shipboard lasers also have potential limitations for countering such targets. Potential advantages and limitations are discussed below.

Advantages

Potential advantages of shipboard lasers for countering surface, air, and ballistic missile targets include the following:

- **Low marginal cost per shot.** Shipboard lasers could counter surface, air, and ballistic missile targets at a low marginal cost per shot. The shipboard fuel needed to generate the electricity for firing an electrically powered laser would cost less than a dollar per shot (some sources express the cost in pennies per shot).[7] In contrast, the Navy's short-range air-defense interceptor missiles cost roughly $800,000 to $1.4 million each, and its longer-range air- and missile-defense interceptor missiles cost several million dollars each.[8] A laser can give a ship an alternative to using an expensive interceptor missile to achieve a "hard kill"[9] against a much less expensive target, such as an unsophisticated unmanned air vehicle (UAV). A low marginal cost per shot could permit the Navy to dramatically improve the cost exchange ratio—the cost of the attacker's weapon compared to the Navy's marginal cost per shot for countering that weapon. Cost exchange ratios currently often favor the attacker, sometimes very significantly. Converting unfavorable cost exchange ratios into favorable ones could be critical for the Navy's ability in coming years to mount an affordable defense against adversaries that choose to deploy large numbers of small boats, UAVs, anti-ship cruise missiles (ASCMs), and ASBMs for possible use against U.S. Navy ships.
- **Deep magazine.** Navy surface ships can carry finite numbers of interceptor missiles in their missile launch tubes. Once a Navy surface ship's interceptors are fired, loading a new set of interceptors onto the ship would require the ship to temporarily withdraw from the battle.

The Phalanx Close-In Weapon System (CIWS) that is installed on Navy surface ships—a radar-controlled Gatling gun that fires bursts of 20mm shells—similarly can engage a finite number of targets before it needs to be reloaded, which takes a certain amount of time. In contrast, an electrically powered laser can be fired again and again, as long as the ship has fuel to generate electricity (and sufficient cooling capacity to remove waste heat from the laser). A laser would give a ship a weapon with a deep (some observers say virtually unlimited) magazine capacity. Lasers could permit Navy surface ships to more effectively defend themselves against adversaries with more weapons and decoys than can be handled by the ships' onboard supplies of interceptor missiles and CIWS ammunition. A ship equipped with a laser, for example, could use the laser to counter an initial wave of decoys while conserving the ship's finite supply of interceptor missiles and CIWS ammunition for incoming weapons that are best countered by those systems. Future ships designed with a combination of lasers and missile-launch tubes could be smaller, and thus less expensive to procure, than future ships designed with no lasers and a larger number of missile-launch tubes.

- **Fast engagement times.** Light from a laser beam can reach a target almost instantly (eliminating the need to calculate an intercept course, as there is with interceptor missiles) and, by remaining focused on a particular spot on the target, cause disabling damage to the target within seconds. After disabling one target, a laser can be redirected in several seconds to another target. Fast engagement times can be particularly important in situations, such as near-shore operations, where missiles, rockets, artillery shells, and mortars could be fired at Navy ships from relatively close distances.
- **Ability to counter radically maneuvering air targets.** Lasers can follow and maintain their beam on radically maneuvering air targets (such as certain ASCMs) that might stress the maneuvering capabilities of Navy interceptor missiles.
- **Precision engagement and reduced risk of certain kinds of collateral damage in port areas.** Lasers are precision-engagement weapons—the light spot from a laser, which might be several inches in diameter, affects what it hits, while generally not affecting (at least not directly) separate nearby objects. Navy ships in overseas ports might be restricted in their ability to use the CIWS to defend themselves against mortars and rockets out of concern that CIWS

shells that are fired upward but miss the target would eventually come back down, possibly causing collateral damage in the port area. In contrast, light from an upward-pointing laser that does not hit the target would continue flying upward in a straight line, which can reduce the chance of causing collateral damage to the port area.

- **Additional uses; graduated responses.** Lasers can perform functions other than destroying targets, including detecting and monitoring targets and producing non-lethal effects, including reversible jamming of electro-optic (EO) sensors.[10] Lasers offer the potential for graduated responses that range from warning targets to reversibly jamming their systems, to causing limited but not disabling damage (as a further warning), and then finally causing disabling damage.

Limitations

Potential limitations of shipboard lasers for countering surface, air, and ballistic missile targets include the following:

- **Line of sight.** Since laser light tends to fly through the atmosphere on an essentially straight path, shipboard lasers would be limited to line-of-sight engagements, and consequently could not counter over-the-horizon targets or targets that are obscured by intervening objects. This limits in particular potential engagement ranges against small boats, which can be obscured by higher waves, or low-flying targets. Even so, lasers can rapidly reacquire boats obscured by periodic swells, and more generally might be able to engage targets at longer ranges than certain existing shipboard gun systems. An airborne mirror, perhaps mounted on an aerostat,[11] could bounce light from a shipboard laser, so as to permit non-line-of-sight engagements; implementing such an arrangement would add cost and technical challenges, and the aerostat could be damaged by a misaimed shipboard laser or enemy attack.
- **Atmospheric absorption, scattering, and turbulence; not an all-weather solution.** Substances in the atmosphere—particularly water vapor, but also things such as sand, dust, salt particles, smoke, and other air pollution—absorb and scatter light from a shipboard laser, and atmospheric turbulence can defocus a laser beam. These effects can reduce the effective range of a laser. Absorption by water vapor is a particular consideration for shipboard lasers because marine environments feature substantial amounts of water vapor in the air.[12]

There are certain wavelengths of light (i.e., "sweet spots" in the electromagnetic spectrum) where atmospheric absorption by water vapor is markedly reduced.[13] Lasers can be designed to emit light at or near those sweet spots, so as to maximize their potential effectiveness. Absorption generally grows with distance to target, making it in general less of a potential problem for short-range operations than for longer-range operations. Adaptive optics, which make rapid, fine adjustments to a laser beam on a continuous basis in response to observed turbulence, can counteract the effects of atmospheric turbulence. Even so, lasers might not work well, or at all, in rain or fog, preventing lasers from being an all-weather solution.

- **Thermal blooming.** A laser that continues firing in the same exact direction for a certain amount of time can heat up the air it is passing through, which in turn can defocus the laser beam, reducing its ability to disable the intended target. This effect, called thermal blooming, can make lasers less effective for countering targets that are coming straight at the ship, on a constant bearing (i.e., "down-thethroat" shots). Other ship self-defense systems, such as interceptor missiles or a CIWS, might be more suitable for countering such targets. Most tests of laser systems have been against crossing targets rather than "down-the-throat" shots. In general, thermal blooming becomes more of a concern as the power of the laser beam increases.

- **Saturation attacks.** Since a laser can attack only one target at a time, requires several seconds to disable it, and several more seconds to be redirected to the next target, a laser can disable only so many targets within a given period of time. This places an upper limit on the ability of an individual laser to deal with saturation attacks—attacks by multiple weapons that approach the ship simultaneously or within a few seconds of one another. This limitation can be mitigated by installing more than one laser on the ship, similar to how the Navy installs multiple CIWS systems on certain ships.[14]

- **Hardened targets and countermeasures.** Less-powerful lasers—that is, lasers with beam powers measured in kilowatts (kW) rather than megawatts (MW)[15]— can have less effectiveness against targets that incorporate shielding, ablative material, or highly reflective surfaces, or that rotate rapidly (so that the laser spot does not remain continuously on a single location on the target's surface) or tumble. Small boats could employ smoke or other obscurants to reduce their susceptibility to laser attack. Measures such as these, however, can

increase the cost and/or weight of a weapon, and obscurants could make it more difficult for small boat operators to see what is around them, reducing their ability to use their boats effectively.
- **Risk of collateral damage to aircraft and satellites.** Since light from an upward-pointing laser that does not hit the target would continue flying upward in a straight line, it could pose a risk of causing unwanted collateral damage to aircraft and satellites.[16]

In addition to the above points, a shipboard laser, like other shipboard systems, would take up space on a ship, use up some of the ship's weight-carrying capacity, create a load on the ship's electrical power and cooling systems, and possibly alter the ship's radar cross section. These considerations—referred to collectively as ship impact—can become significant when considering whether to backfit lasers onto existing ships, or whether to incorporate lasers into new ship designs.[17]

Potential Targets for Shipboard Lasers
Potential targets for shipboard lasers include the following:

- electro-optical (EO) sensors, including those on anti-ship missiles;
- small boats (including so-called "swarm boats")[18] and other watercraft (such as jet skis);
- rockets, artillery shells, mortars (sometimes collectively referred to as RAM);
- UAVs;
- manned aircraft;
- ASCMs; and
- ballistic missiles, including ASBMs.

Small boats, rockets, artillery shells, and mortars can be a particular concern for Navy surface ships during operations close to shore. Iran has acquired large numbers of swarm boats for potential use during a crisis or conflict against U.S. Navy ships seeking to enter or operate in the Persian Gulf. RAM weapons are widely proliferated to both state and non-state organizations. UAVs, including relatively simple and inexpensive models, can be used to collect and transmit targeting data on Navy ships, attack Navy ships directly by diving into them, and be armed to attack Navy ships at a distance. ASCMs are widely proliferated to state actors, and were also reportedly used by the non-state Hezbollah organization in 2006 to attack an Israeli warship.

As mentioned earlier, China is believed to be developing an ASBM. Lasers that are not capable of disabling ballistic missiles could nevertheless augment ballistic missile defense operations by being used for precision tracking and imaging.

Required Laser Power Levels for Countering Targets

A laser's ability to disable a target depends in large part on the power and beam quality of its light beam. The power of the light beam is measured in kilowatts (kW) or megawatts (MW). Beam quality (BQ) is a measure of how well focused the beam is.[19] Additional factors affecting a laser's ability to disable a target include:

- atmospheric absorption, scattering, and turbulence,[20]
- jitter—the degree to which the spot of laser light jumps around on the surface of the target due to vibration or other movement of the laser system,[21] and
- target design features, which can affect a target's susceptibility to laser damage.

Table B-1 in Appendix B summarizes some government and industry perspectives regarding power levels needed to counter certain targets. Although these perspectives differ somewhat, the following conclusions might be drawn from the table regarding approximate laser power levels needed to affect certain targets:

- **Lasers with a power level of about 10 kW** might be able to counter some UAVs at short range, particularly "soft" UAVs (i.e., those with design features that make them particularly susceptible to laser damage).
- **Lasers with power levels in the tens of kilowatts** could have more capability for countering UAVs, and could counter at least some small boats as well.
- **Lasers with a power level of about 100 kW** would have a greater ability for countering UAVs and small boats, as well as some capability for countering rockets, artillery, and mortars.
- **Lasers with power levels in the hundreds of kilowatts** could have greater ability for countering targets mentioned above, and could also counter manned aircraft and some missiles.

- **Lasers with power levels in the megawatts** could have greater ability for countering targets mentioned above—including supersonic ASCMs and ballistic missiles—at ranges of up to about 10 nautical miles.

In addition to the points above, one Navy briefing stated that lasers with power levels above 300 kW could permit a ship to defend not only itself, but other ships in the area as well (a capability referred to as area defense or escort operations or battle group operations).

Types of Lasers Being Developed for Potential Shipboard Use

The Navy and DOD are developing three principal types of lasers for potential use on Navy surface ships:

- fiber solid state lasers (SSLs),
- slab SSLs, and
- free electron lasers (FELs).

All three types are electrically powered.[22] Each type is discussed briefly below. Additional information on each type is presented in **Appendix D**, **Appendix E**, and **Appendix F**.

Fiber Solid State Lasers (Fiber SSLs)

Fiber solid state lasers (SSLs) are widely used in industry—tens of thousands are used by auto and truck manufacturing firms for cutting and welding metal. Consequently, they are considered to be a very robust technology. The Navy's fiber SSL prototype demonstrator, called the **Laser Weapon System (LaWS)**, has a beam power of 33 kW. The Navy envisions LaWS being used for operations such as disabling or reversibly jamming EO sensors, countering UAVs and EO guided missiles, and augmenting radar tracking. The Navy envisions installing LaWS on a ship either on its own mount or (more likely) as an add-on to an existing Phalanx Close-In Weapon System (CIWS) mount.[23] The Navy is currently working on integrating LaWS with CIWS, to support the latter option.

The Navy states the following regarding tests of LaWS:

- In June 2009, LaWS successfully engaged five threat-representative UAVs[24] in five attempts in tests in combat-representative scenarios in a desert setting at the Naval Air Weapons Station at China Lake, in southern California
- In May 2010, LaWS successfully engaged four threat-representative UAVs in four attempts in combat-representative scenarios at a range of about one nautical mile in an over-the-water setting conducted from San Nicholas Island, off the coast of southern California. LaWS during these tests also demonstrated an ability to destroy materials used in rigid-hull inflatable boats (RHIBs—a type of small boat) at a range of about half a nautical mile, and to reversibly jam and disrupt electro-optical/infrared sensors.[25]

The Navy is currently working on scaling up the power of the LaWS beam to about 100 kW by FY2014. How much beyond 100 kW the system could eventually be scaled up to is not clear, but the system is not generally viewed as having the potential for being scaled up to megawatt power levels.

The Navy states that as of December 2010, LaWS was at a Technology Readiness Level (TRL) of 5, meaning component and/or breadboard validation in a relevant environment.[26] The Navy estimates that it might cost roughly $150 million to develop LaWS to TRL 7, meaning the demonstration of a system prototype in an operational environment. The Navy considers the LaWS effort to be ready for conversion into a program of record, should policymakers decide that this would be desirable. If the LaWS effort were converted soon into a POR, the Navy believes a production version of LaWS might achieve Initial Operational Capability (or IOC—a type of official in-service date) on Navy surface ships around FY2017. The Navy estimates that production copies of the LaWS system could be installed and procured as additions to ship CIWS mounts for a total cost roughly $17 million per CIWS mount.[27]

For additional information on fiber SSLs and LaWS, see **Appendix D**.

Slab Solid State Lasers (Slab SSLs)

DOD has pursued multiple efforts to develop slab SSLs for military use. Among these is the **Maritime Laser Demonstration (MLD)**, a prototype laser weapon developed as a rapid demonstration project under DOD's Joint High Power SSL (JHPSSL) program. MLD leverages development work on slab SSLs done elsewhere in DOD under the JHPSSL program. In March 2009, Northrop demonstrated a version of MLD that coherently combined seven slab SSLs, each with a power of about 15 kW, to create a beam with a power of about 105 kW.

In July 2010, the ability of MLD to track small boats in a marine environment was tested at NSWC Port Hueneme, CA.[28] In late August and early September 2010, MLD was tested in an over-the-water setting at the Navy's Potomac River Test Range against stationary targets, including representative small boat sections.[29] In November 2010, an at-sea test of the system against small boat targets reportedly was stopped midway because one of the system's components needed to be replaced.[30]

Scaling up a slab laser to a total power of 300 kW is not considered to require any technological breakthroughs. Supporters of slab SSLs such as MLD believe they could eventually be scaled up further, to perhaps 600 kW. Slab SSLs are not generally viewed as easily scalable to megawatt power levels.

The Navy states that as of December 2010, MLD was at a Technology Readiness Level (TRL) of 5, meaning component and/or breadboard validation in a relevant environment.[31]

For additional information on slab SSLs and MLD, see **Appendix E**.

Free Electron Lasers (FELs)

Unlike slab SSLs, which are being developed by multiple U.S. military services, FELs are being developed within DOD solely by the Navy, in part because they would be too large to be installed on Army or Marine Corps ground vehicles or Air Force tactical aircraft, and in part because an FEL's ability to change its wavelength so as to match atmospheric transmission sweet spots makes it particularly suited for operations in a marine environment. The basic architecture of an FEL offers a clear potential for scaling up to power levels of one or more megawatts.

A 14.7 kW FEL has been developed; it has not been moved out of a laboratory setting or fired at an operational moving target. ONR is now funding the development, as an Innovative Naval Prototype (INP),[32] of a 100 kW FEL; the work is scheduled to be performed during FY2010- FY2015.[33] Developing a 100 kW FEL reduces the risks associated with developing a megawatt-class FEL. If a decision were made to develop a megawatt-class FEL for incorporation as a shipboard weapon, the Navy believes the development work could occur during FY2016- FY2021.

The Navy states that as of December 2010, FEL was at a Technology Readiness Level (TRL) of 4 (meaning component and/or breadboard validation in a laboratory environment).[34]

For additional information on FEL, see **Appendix F**.

Remaining Technical Challenges

Navy and DOD research on military lasers has overcome many of the technical challenges associated with developing shipboard lasers, but a number of challenges remain. As mentioned in the preceding sections, the Navy states that as of December 2010, LaWS and MLD were at a Technology Readiness Level (TRL) of 5 (meaning component and/or breadboard validation in a relevant environment) and that FEL was at a TRL of 4 (meaning component and/or breadboard validation in a laboratory environment).

Remaining technical challenges for potential shipboard lasers can be grouped into four broad categories:

- scaling up beam power to higher levels while maintaining or improving beam quality and addressing thermal management (the removal of waste heat from the gain medium);
- turning prototype and demonstration versions of lasers into versions that are suitable for series production, shipboard installation, and shipboard operation and maintenance over many years of use;
- engineering other parts of a complete laser weapon system, including target detection and tracking, and beam pointing; and
- integrating lasers with ship power and cooling systems, and with ship combat systems (i.e., a ship's integrated collection of sensors, computers, displays, and weapons).

Although these challenges are stated briefly here, they are not trivial. Skeptics might argue that certain past DOD laser development efforts proved over-optimistic in terms of projections for overcoming technical challenges and producing operational weapons. In spite of decades of development work, these skeptics might note, DOD has not deployed an operational high-energy laser weapon system.

Scaling up beam power to megawatt levels is a principal challenge at this point for the FEL. ONR believes that scaling up FEL from 14 kW to 100 kW will make it substantially easier to then scale up FEL to megawatt power levels. Thermal management is a particular challenge for SSLs. (Supporters of fiber SSLs say it is less of a challenge for fiber SSLs than for slab SSLs.) Supporters of LaWS argue that many of the challenges associated with fielding the system have been overcome; a May 11, 2010, press report states:

> Taking a laser weapon from land to sea presents a few challenges, [Capt. Dave Kiel, Naval Sea Systems Command directed energy and electric weapons program manager] said. "To me, all the technical challenges that exist to moving to a maritime environment are really just engineering issues. I don't think there will be any significant S&T [science and technology] issues."
>
> The issues range from stabilizing the system to the effect that higher humidity has on absorbing some of a lasers power as it passes through the atmosphere, he said.
>
> "The biggest issues though aren't purely technical they are related to just the whole socialization issue—no one has ever had a laser weapon on a ship before and it is going to take people time to get used to them," Kiel added.[35]
>
> That means making sure the laser does what it is advertised to do and that every time the system is turned on, no one is going to be blinded from the laser, he said.[36]

Navy Surface Fleet's Generalized Vision for Shipboard Lasers

The Navy's surface fleet has a generalized vision for shipboard lasers that envisages deploying lasers into the current Navy, the "Next Navy" (i.e., the Navy that will be produced by current shipbuilding programs), and the "Navy After Next" (i.e., the Navy that will be produced by future shipbuilding programs). This generalized vision can be summarized as follows (text based on a Navy briefing slide):

- **Current Navy—LaWs:**
    - 50 kw to 100 kW fiber laser with a low beam quality (BQ)[37] and a beam director with a diameter of about 60 cm (about 23.6 inches);
    - short-range operations against targets such as EO sensors, small boats, UAVs; RAM; and man-portable air defense systems (or MANPADs— shoulder-fired surface-to-air missiles);[38]
    - potential IOC around FY2017;

- **Next Navy:**
  - 100 kW laser with a BQ of about 2 and use of adaptive optics;
    - Extended-range operations against targets such as EO sensors, small boats, UAVs, RAM, and MANPADs, as well as ASCMs that are flying on a crossing path (rather than at the ship);
- **Navy After Next—FEL:**
  - 1 MW FEL laser using a beam director with a diameter of more than 1 meter (more than about 39 inches);
  - Self-defense operations against transonic and supersonic/highly maneuverable anti-ship missiles, and ballistic missiles.

Although this generalized vision refers to laser types and specifications and generalized time frames for installing lasers on Navy ships, it is not a program of record for procuring a production version of a shipboard laser, or a roadmap that calls for installing lasers on specific surface ships by specific dates. The Navy currently does not have such a program of record or roadmap.

ISSUES FOR CONGRESS

Program of Record and Roadmap

Although the Navy is developing laser technologies and prototypes of potential shipboard lasers, and has a generalized vision for shipboard lasers (see "Navy Surface Fleet's Generalized Vision for Shipboard Lasers"), the Navy does not have a program of record for procuring a production version of a shipboard laser, or a roadmap that calls for installing lasers on specific surface ships by specific dates. The Navy states that it is taking a measured approach toward the development and implementation of lasers (and other directed energy weapons) that includes, among other things, developing and testing prototype and demonstration lasers and monitoring independent laser experiments performed by commercial firms. Current operational requirements, the Navy states, do not specify shipboard directed energy weapons to address capability gaps. The Navy states that although lasers and other directed-energy weapons offer options for providing required capabilities, a business case for directed energy weapons over traditional kinetic weapons (such as guns and missiles) has not been developed. The Navy states that although it has not performed an analysis of alternatives (AOA) comparing directed energy weapons to traditional kinetic energy weapons, it is continually analyzing its defensive capabilities for effectiveness against current and potential future threats.

One potential issue for Congress is whether the Navy should act now to adopt a program of record for procuring a production version of a shipboard laser, and/or a roadmap that calls for installing lasers on specific surface ships by specific dates.

Regarding the possibility of developing a roadmap for shipboard lasers, it can be noted that the Navy in recent years has developed or called for the development of roadmaps or master plans in a number of other technology and policy areas, including the Navy's future computing and information environment,[39] information dominance,[40] UAVs,[41] unmanned underwater vehicles (UUVs),[42] unmanned surface vehicles (USVs),[43] the Navy's response to changing conditions in the Arctic,[44] the Navy's response to climate change,[45] and military transformation of the Navy.[46]

Arguments Against Developing a Roadmap or Program of Record

Supporters of the current Navy approach of not acting now to adopt a program of record for procuring a production version of a shipboard laser and/or a roadmap that calls for installing lasers on specific surface ships by specific dates could argue one or more of the following:

- **Operational requirements and business case.** Current Navy operational requirements do not specify shipboard directed energy weapons to address capability gaps, and the Navy has not developed a business case for directed energy weapons over traditional kinetic weapons (such as guns and missiles). Until these two things change, it would be premature to adopt a program of record for procuring a production version of a shipboard laser or a roadmap that calls for installing lasers on specific surface ships by specific dates.
- **State of development and risk of "rush to failure."** The current state of development of potential shipboard lasers includes significant unresolved questions about, for example, how far beam power can be scaled up while maintaining or improving beam quality and handling thermal management issues. In light of these questions, committing

the Navy now to deploying lasers on specific ships by specific dates would be premature, and could lead to a "rush to failure" in the Navy's shipboard laser efforts.

- **Flexibility to incorporate advances.** The Navy's approach of not committing now to installing lasers on specific ships by specific dates is appropriate in light of the rapid rate of advance in SSL technologies in recent years. The Navy's current approach is a flexible strategy that allows these advances to be folded into the Navy's effort as they occur, often at little or no cost to the Navy. Committing now to installing lasers on specific ships by specific dates could lock the Navy into a laser design that might quickly be made obsolete by such advances.
- **History of overly optimistic promises on other DOD lasers.** The Navy's current approach of not committing now to installing lasers on specific ships by specific dates reflects lessons learned from past DOD laser development efforts, which include promises concerning the potential dates for having lasers enter operational service that later proved to be overly optimistic.
- **Socialization.** The Navy's current approach allows time for lasers to become properly "socialized" within the Navy—that is, for knowledge of, and comfort with, lasers to become more widespread among Navy personnel. Committing now to installing lasers on specific ships by specific dates could result in lasers being installed on ships before adequate socialization of lasers within the Navy occurs. This could lead to institutional resistance to, and rejection of, lasers by the broader Navy community.

Arguments Supporting Developing a Roadmap or Program of Record

Those who support having the Navy act now to adopt a program of record for procuring a production version of a shipboard laser and/or a roadmap that calls for installing lasers on specific surface ships by specific dates could argue one or more of the following:

- **Operational requirements and business case.** Current Navy operational requirements documents can be outdated or reflect insufficient familiarity or comfort with a new technology. Shipboard lasers are caught in a "Catch-22" dilemma traditionally faced by new and different weapon technologies: Operational requirements or a business case for installing shipboard lasers would be best made on the basis of a thorough understanding of the potential uses and value of shipboard lasers, but such an understanding cannot be developed until lasers are installed on ships and used by Navy personnel in various operational settings. In addition, new technologies are often less efficient or less cost effective in their initial versions than they are in later versions, but deploying initial versions can speed up the process of developing follow-on versions that are more efficient or cost effective. Developing a roadmap or program of record could help overcome this dilemma, encourage the Navy to "get off the dime" on procuring and installing shipboard lasers, and prevent shipboard lasers from being perpetually stuck in the research and development stage (i.e., a "technology sandbox").

- **State of development and risk of "rush to failure."** Supporters of LaWS believe it is ready for conversion into a program of record. Supporters of MLD argue similarly argue that MLD is ready for conversion into a program of record. A roadmap or program of record can include realistic installation dates that avoid creating a risk of a "rush to failure."
- **Flexibility to incorporate advances.** A roadmap or program of record can include features that provide flexibility for incorporating technology advancements as they occur. DOD's approach of evolutionary acquisition with spiral development, which DOD adopted in 2001 as its standard acquisition approach, is intended to permit this.[47]
- **History of overly optimistic promises on other DOD lasers.** The best way to overcome the history of overly optimistic promises on DOD laser-development efforts is to develop, adopt, and successfully implement a roadmap or program of record for installing lasers on specific ships by specific dates that includes realistic goals for the capabilities of the lasers to be installed and realistic installation dates.
- **Socialization.** The best way to socialize shipboard lasers within the broader Navy community is to install them on Navy ships and permit Navy personnel to use them. As long as lasers remain primarily in the research and development arena, socialization of lasers among the boarder Navy community will occur slowly, if at all.

Past studies on military lasers in general, including potential shipboard lasers, include comments bearing on the above debate. A 2005 Northrop paper, for example, stated:

Despite these technical advances in laser weapons, much of the military operational community remains unaware of their potential. Numerous discussions with serving officers at seminars, conferences and wargames over the past several years indicate that understanding of the current state of progress in laser weapons is mostly limited to the scientific and technical communities. Beyond that, even the leading thinkers and writers of the military operational community have paid scarce attention to laser weapons and their operational implications.... Despite several nascent efforts to understand the military worth of these systems, appreciation of their potential throughout the military operational community remains low.[48]

The paper also stated:

Solid-state and free-electron laser weapons, adding to the range of laser weapons capabilities, may be less than a decade away. Meanwhile, the personnel who will make key decisions on the development, acquisition and employment of these systems are already halfway or more through their military careers but most have developed little awareness of the potential implications of laser weapons.[49]

The chairman of the Defense Science Board (DSB), in a cover memorandum to a 2007 DSB task force report on directed energy weapon systems and technology applications, stated: "Even after many years of development, there is not a single directed energy system fielded today, and fewer programs of record exist today than in 2001. This circumstance is unlikely to change without a renewed focus on this important area."[50] The co-chairs of the task force, in their own cover memorandum to the report, stated that

Directed energy offers promise as a transformational "game changer" in military operations, able to augment and improve operational capabilities in many areas. Yet despite this potential, years of investment have not resulted in any operational systems with higher energy laser capability. The lack of progress is a result of many factors from unexpected technical challenges to a lack of understanding of the costs and benefits of such systems. Ultimately, as a result of these circumstances, interest in such systems has declined over the years.[51]

The task force's report states that

> The most fundamental issue affecting priority for developing and fielding laser and microwave/millimeter system useful to combatant command missions is the need for cost-benefit analyses supporting priority choices....
>
> [H]istorically, the US military has often been slow to identify, adequately prioritize, and respond effectively to the emerging challenges likely to impose the greatest stresses on our forces in future contingencies....
>
> Insofar as directed-energy weapons do not address current operational problems such as combating insurgents and terrorists in Iraq or Afghanistan, and to the extent that they promise to disrupt ways of fighting with which the US military Services are comfortable or to threaten dominant subcultures within these institutions, there may be considerable resistance to this new class of weaponry from the warfighters.[54]

The paper also states:

> CSBA's analysis of the prospects for achieving a 2018 IOC [Initial Operational Capability] [for battlefield lasers] has ascertained that a significant number of perceptual, fiscal, operational and institutional obstacles would have to be addressed before fielding is likely to take place. To begin with, there is a history of unfulfilled promises regarding high-energy laser (HEL) technologies from the directed energy community that extends back to the 1970s. The danger, of course, is that this poor past performance could lead decision-makers to downplay or ignore recent advances in laser technologies that, if pursued, could finally yield battlefield applications.[55]

Number of Laser Types to Continue Developing

Potential Strategies

A second potential issue for Congress is how many of the three laser types discussed in this report—fiber SSLs, slab SSLs, and FELs—the Navy should continue developing.

Supporters of stopping development of all three types (or of continuing development of one type) might argue that continuing the development of shipboard lasers (or of more than one type of laser), while perhaps desirable, would reduce funding for more important Navy program priorities below critical levels, particularly in a situation of constrained Navy resources. They might argue that the Navy's kinetic weapons in coming years will have sufficient (or largely sufficient) capability for countering the kinds of targets that shipboard lasers could counter.

Supporters of continuing development of two or three types might argue that it would permit continued competition between laser types and provide a hedge against the failure of one of the development efforts. DOD in the past, they might argue, has sometimes pursued comparable programs concurrently to ensure the best outcome for an area of effort deemed important. They might also argue that the Navy's kinetic weapons in coming years will be insufficient to counter certain kinds of targets, or that shipboard lasers would counter them more cost effectively.

Relative Merits of Laser Types

In considering which laser types to continue developing, policymakers may consider the relative merits of each type. Below are some arguments relating to the relative merits each type. The discussions below are intended as introductory only; a full comparison of their relative merits would entail much longer discussions.

Some Arguments Relating to Fiber SSLs

Supporters of LaWS argue that it has a demonstrated ability to counter certain targets of interest at short (but tactically useful) ranges in a marine environment; that it can be installed on Navy ships in the near term; that it promises to be less expensive than a slab SSL; that it poses less of a challenge in terms of thermal management than a slab SSL; that it has less ship impact than FELs; that it uses an industrial laser technology with high reliability and few alignment optics, making possible a simplified system engineering solution for a Navy laser system; and that its power can be scaled up to 100 kW or perhaps more. They argue that the system's BQ, though not excellent, is good enough to disable targets of interest at short ranges. They argue that the system's light wavelength of 1.064 microns, though not exactly on the atmospheric transmission "sweet spot" located at 1.045 microns, is good enough in terms of atmospheric transmission to permit the laser to disable targets of interest at tactically useful ranges, and that development work is underway on SSLs that would emit light at wavelengths above the threshold (about 1.5 microns) at which laser light becomes much less dangerous to human eyes.

Some skeptics of LaWS, including supporters of the MLD, argue that the LaWS's BQ limits its effective range. Other skeptics of LaWS, including supporters of FELs, argue that LaWS's operating wavelength limits its effective range, particularly when compared to FELs, whose wavelengths can be tuned to exactly match atmospheric transmission sweet spots, and that LaWS's current wavelength is dangerous to human eyes, whereas an FEL can operate at wavelengths matching atmospheric sweet spots that are located above 1.5 microns.

Some Arguments Relating to Slab SSLs

Supporters of MLD argue that it has a demonstrated power level of 105 kW (more than three times that of LaWS); that it has a much better BQ than LaWS, permitting it to counter targets at greater ranges (thereby providing a larger defended area around the ship, and more time to counter targets approaching the ship); that it could be ready for installation on ships as soon as, or not very long after, the LaWS system would be; that a production version could have a procurement cost comparable to, or even less than, that of a production version of LaWS; that the challenge slab SSLs pose in terms of thermal management, though perhaps greater than that of fiber SSLs, can nevertheless be handled; and that slab SSLs can be scaled up to 300 kW or more while retaining good BQ. The MLD contract, they argue, was competitively awarded, that the competitors for the contract included fiber SSLs, and that the contract was awarded instead to a slab SSL.

Supporters of slab MLDs argue that the difference in complexity between fiber SSLs and slab SSLs is not as great as some supporters of LaWS contend—that fiber SSLs, for example, have more free-space optics[56] than slab SSLs. Supporters of MLD argue that the industrial environments in which commercial fiber SSLs have operated are not characterized by shocks or high humidity—two features that characterize the shipboard operating environment—whereas MLD was designed from the start with eventual ship operations in mind. Supporters of MLD argue that it can be maintained easily in the field through the use of sealed line replaceable units (LRUs).[57] MLD supporters argue, as do supporters of LaWS, that the system has less ship impact than an FEL; that system's light wavelength of 1.064 microns, though not exactly on the atmospheric transmission "sweet spot" located at 1.045 microns, is good enough in terms of atmospheric transmission to permit the laser to disable targets of interest at tactically useful ranges, and that development work is underway on SSLs that would emit light at wavelengths above the threshold (about 1.5 microns) at which laser light becomes much less dangerous to human eyes.

Skeptics of MLD, including supporters of LaWS, argue that it uses complex optics, making it more expensive to procure and potentially less reliable and more difficult to maintain than LaWS. Other skeptics of MLD, including supporters of FELs, argue, as they do regarding LaWS, that MLD's operating wavelength limits its effective range, particularly when compared to FELs, whose wavelengths can be tuned to exactly match atmospheric transmission sweet spots, and that MLD's current wavelength is dangerous to human eyes, whereas an FEL can operate at wavelengths matching atmospheric sweet spots that are located above 1.5 microns.

Some Arguments Relating to FELs

Supporters of FELs argue that unlike SSLs, FELs clearly can be scaled up to megawatt power levels that would be capable of countering a wide range of targets, including supersonic ASCMs and ballistic missiles, and that unlike SSLs, FELs can be scaled up in power from 10 kW to 1 MW without any increase in the size of the system or need for a beam combiner (a component that adds to system complexity and cost). Supporters of FELs argue that in contrast to the fixed wavelength of light emitted by an SSL, the wavelength of light emitted by an FEL can be tuned to exactly match various atmospheric transmission sweet spots, including those above the threshold (about 1.5 microns) at which laser light becomes much less dangerous to human eyes. They also argue that in contrast to SSLs, FELs pose no large thermal management issues because an FEL's waste heat is not produced inside the laser mechanism itself.

Skeptics of FELs, including supporters of SSLs, argue that FELs will not be ready for installation on ships for a significant number of years. They argue that FELs are so large that they cannot be incorporated into most if not all existing Navy ship designs, limiting the potential applicability of FELs to the surface fleet for many years, and that incorporating an FEL into a new ship design could make the ship considerably larger, adding to the ship's construction cost. They also argue that the need for isolating the FEL system from vibration and shock and the possible need for using cryogenic equipment adds to an FEL's cost and complexity.

Implications for Ship Design and Acquisition

Another potential issue for Congress are the possible implications that shipboard lasers might have for the design and acquisition of Navy ships, including the Flight III DDG-51 destroyer that the Navy wants to begin procuring in FY2016.[58] The ability of existing Navy ship designs to support lasers, particularly in terms of having sufficient electrical power and cooling capacity, can be summarized as follows:

- The Navy has concluded that its Aegis cruisers and destroyers (i.e., CG-47 and DDG-51 class ships), as well as San Antonio (LPD-17) class amphibious ships, would have enough available electrical power under battle conditions (i.e., when many other systems are also drawing electrical power) to support a LaWS system. An August 2010 press report stated: "Today's warships have enough power to support a 100-kilowatt laser, said [Capt. David Kiel, program manager for directed energy and electric weapons at Naval Sea Systems Command]. Any surface combatant large enough to accommodate the close-in weapon system [CIWS] could also carry the fiber laser, he added."[59]
- Some Navy ships might be able to support, under battle conditions, an SSL with a power *somewhat* above 100 kW.
- No existing Navy surface combatant designs have enough electrical power or cooling capacity to support an SSL with a power level *well* above 100 kW.
- Because of its probable size, an FEL could not be backfitted onto existing cruisers or destroyers. Aircraft carriers and "large-deck" amphibious assault ships (i.e., LHA/LHD-type amphibious ships) might have enough room to accommodate an FEL, but existing carriers and amphibious assault ships might not have enough electrical power to support a megawatt-class FEL. In addition, because of thermal blooming and the status of carriers and amphibious assault ships as potential high-value targets, it might make more operational sense to install megawatt-class FELs on ships other than carriers or amphibious assault ships.[60]

The above points suggest that the Navy in coming years could face significant ship-design constraints in its ability to install shipboard lasers, particularly SSLs well above 100 kW in power, and FELs in general. These constraints are a product, in part, of the Navy's termination of the CG(X) cruiser program, because the CG(X) could have been designed to support SSLs well above 100 kW in power and/or a megawatt-class FEL.[61] Following the termination of the CG(X) program, the Navy has no announced plans to acquire a surface combatant clearly capable of supporting an SSL well above 100 kW in power, or an FEL.

Ship-design options for expanding the Navy's ability to install lasers on its surface ships in coming years include the following:

- design the new Flight III version of the DDG-51 destroyer, which the Navy wants to start procuring in FY2016, with enough space, electrical power, and cooling capacity to support an SSL with a power level of 200 kW or 300 kW or more—something that could require lengthening the DDG-51 hull, so as to provide room for laser equipment and additional electrical generating and cooling equipment;
- design and procure a new destroyer as a follow-on or substitute for the Flight III DDG-51 that can support an SSL with a power level of 200 kW or 300 kW or more, and/or a megawatt-class FEL;[62] and
- modify the designs of amphibious assault ships to be procured in coming years, so that they can support SSLs with power levels of 200 kW or 300 kW or more, and/or megawatt-class FELs; and
- modify the design of the Navy's new Ford (CVN-78) class aircraft carriers, if necessary, so that they can support SSLs with power levels of 200 kW or 300 kW or more, and/or megawatt-class FELs.[63]

OPTIONS FOR CONGRESS

Congress in past years has provided some additional funding to help support Navy development of potential shipboard lasers. For FY2012 and subsequent years, Congress has several potential options regarding potential shipboard lasers, including the following:

- request additional information from the Navy and DOD about potential shipboard lasers, perhaps by holding one or more hearings on the issue, or by requiring the Navy to submit one or more reports to Congress on the topic;

Navy Shipboard Lasers for Surface, Air, and Missile Defense 27

- approve, reduce, eliminate, or increase the Navy's funding requests for development of potential shipboard lasers;
- encourage or direct the Navy or some other DOD organization to perform an analysis of alternatives (AOA) comparing the cost-effectiveness of lasers and traditional kinetic weapons (such as guns and missiles) for countering surface, air, and missile targets;
- encourage or direct the Navy to adopt a program of record for procuring a production version of a shipboard laser, and/or a roadmap that calls for installing lasers on specific surface ships by specific dates;
- review and comment on any roadmap for shipboard lasers that the Navy adopts;
- in the absence of a Navy program of record or roadmap, direct the Navy to develop and install lasers with certain capabilities on a certain number of Navy surface ships by a certain date;[64]
- encourage or direct the Navy to design the Flight III version of the DDG-51 destroyer so that it can support an SSL with a power level of 200 kW or 300 kW or more;
- encourage or direct the Navy to design and procure a new destroyer as a follow-on or substitute for the Flight III DDG-51 that can support an SSL with a power level of 200 kW or 300 kW or more, and/or a megawatt-class FEL;
- encourage or direct the Navy to modify the designs of amphibious assault ships to be procured in coming years, so that they can support SSLs with power levels of 200 kW or 300 kW or more, and/or megawatt-class FELs; and
- encourage or direct the Navy to modify the design of the Navy's new Ford (CVN-78) class aircraft carriers, if necessary, so that they can support SSLs with power levels of 200 kW or 300 kW or more, and/or megawatt-class FELs.

LEGISLATIVE ACTIVITY FOR FY2012

The Administration is expected to submit its proposed FY2012 defense budget to Congress on or about February 14, 2011.

APPENDIX A. LEGISLATIVE ACTIVITY FOR FY2011

FY2011 Defense Authorization Act (H.R. 6523/P.L. 111-383)

Senate (S. 3454)

Section 144 of S. 3454 as reported by the Senate Armed Services Committee (S.Rept. 111-201 of June 4, 2010) states:

SEC. 144. INTEGRATION OF SOLID STATE LASER SYSTEMS INTO CERTAIN AIRCRAFT.
(a) Analysis of Feasability Required- The Secretary of Defense shall conduct an analysis of the feasability of integrating solid state laser systems into the aircraft platforms specified in subsection (b) for purposes of permitting such aircraft to accomplish their missions, including to provide close air support.
(b) Aircraft- The aircraft platforms specified in this subsection shall include, at a minimum, the following:
The C-130 aircraft.
The B-1 bomber aircraft.
The F-35 fighter aircraft.
(c) Scope of Analysis- The analysis required by subsection (a) shall include a determination of the following:
(1) The estimated cost per unit of each laser system analyzed.
(2) The estimated cost of operation and maintenance of each aircraft platform specified in subsection (b) in connection with each laser system analyzed, noting that the fidelity of such analysis may not be uniform for all aircraft platforms.

S.Rept. 111-201 states the following regarding Section 144:

Integration of solid state laser systems into certain aircraft (sec. 144) The committee notes that the Department of Defense has longstanding research and development programs to advance the military usefulness of high-powered lasers mounted on aircraft for defensive and offensive capabilities. Recent advances in the power and cooling of solid state lasers have led the Department to begin to develop, integrate, and test such lasers on military aircraft such as the B–1 bomber. There is concern that the Department may solely focus on the B–1 platform without fully analyzing the cost-benefit implications as it moves from demonstration to development.
Hence, the committee recommends a provision for the Department to provide to the congressional defense committees no later than February 2011, a report analyzing various candidate aircraft that are

being considered as platforms for high power solid state lasers and provide an estimated unit cost to develop an integrated laser-aircraft system. The analysis should also estimate the operations and maintenance costs of such an integrated laser aircraft system. The committee notes there may not be complete data for some candidate aircraft but asks the Department to begin this analysis as early as possible in order to fully understand long-term life cycle costs. The committee also requests that the analysis of the B-1 should consider the operational placement of the laser in the aft bay so as to maintain the operational kinetic capabilities of the forward and center bays. (Page 18)

Final Version (H.R. 6523/P.L. 111-383)

Section 126 of H.R. 6523/P.L. 111-383 of January 7, 2011, states:

> SEC. 126. INTEGRATION OF SOLID STATE LASER SYSTEMS INTO CERTAIN AIRCRAFT.
> (a) Analysis of Feasibility Required- The Secretary of Defense shall conduct an analysis of the feasibility of integrating solid state laser systems into the aircraft platforms specified in subsection (b) for purposes of permitting such aircraft to accomplish their missions, including to provide close air support.
> (b) Aircraft- The aircraft platforms specified in this subsection shall include, at a minimum, the following:
> The C-130 aircraft.
> The B-1 bomber aircraft.
> The F-35 fighter aircraft.
> (c) Scope of Analysis- The analysis required by subsection (a) shall include a determination of the following:
> (1) The estimated cost per unit of each laser system analyzed.
> (2) The estimated cost of operation and maintenance of each aircraft platform specified in subsection (b) in connection with each laser system analyzed, noting that the fidelity of such analysis may not be uniform for all aircraft platforms.

FY2011 DOD Appropriations Bill (S. 3800)

Senate

The Senate Appropriations Committee, in its report (S.Rept. 111-295 of September 16, 2010) on S. 3800, recommends increasing the Navy's FY2011 request for research and development funding by $2 million for "High Power Laser Technologies Initiative" (page 151, line 73) and by $12 million for "Laser Phalanx" (page 151, line 121).

APPENDIX B. LASER POWER LEVELS REQUIRED TO COUNTER TARGETS

Table B-1 shows two Navy perspectives, a Defense Science Board (DSB) task force perspective, and two industry perspectives on approximate laser power levels needed to affect various categories of targets. As can be seen in the table, these perspectives differ somewhat regarding the power levels needed to counter certain targets, perhaps because of differing assumptions about beam quality (BQ) and other factors.

Table B-1. Approximate Laser Power Levels Needed to Affect Certain Targets

Multiple perspectives that may reflect varying assumptions about BQ and other factors

Source	Beam power measured in kilowatts (kW) or megawatts (MW)			
	~10 kW	Tens of kW	~100 kW	Hundreds of kW	MW
One Navy briefing (2010)	UAVs	Small boats		Missiles (starting at 500 kW)	
Another Navy briefing (2010)		Short-range operations against UAVs, RAM, MANPADS (50 kW-100kW; low BQ)		Extended-range operations against UAVs, RAM, MANPADS, ASCMs flying a crossing path (>100 kW, BQ of ~2)	Operations against supersonic, highly maneuverable ASCMs, transonic air-to-surface missiles, and ballistic missiles (>1 MW)

Table B-1. (Continued).

Source	Beam power measured in kilowatts (kW) or megawatts (MW)			
	~10 kW	Tens of kW	~100 kW	Hundreds of kW	MW

Source	~10 kW	Tens of kW	~100 kW	Hundreds of kW	MW
Industry briefing (2010)		UAVs and small boats (50 kW)	RAM (100+ kW), subsonic ASCMs (300 kW), manned aircraft (500 kW)		Supersonic ASCMs and ballistic missiles
Defense Science Board (DSB) report (2007)		Surface threats at 1-2 km		Ground-based air and missile defense, and countering rockets, artillery, and mortars, at 5-10 km[a]	"Battle group defense" at 5-20 km (1-3 MW)
Northrop Grumman research paper (2005)	Soft UAVs at short range	Aircraft and cruise missiles at short range	Soft UAVs at long range	Aircraft and cruise missiles at long range, and artillery rockets (lower hundreds of kW) Artillery shells and terminal defense against very short range ballistic missiles (higher 100s of kW)	

Source: One Navy briefing: Briefing slide entitled "HEL [High-Energy Laser] Missions," in briefing entitled "Surface Navy Laser Vision," Warfare Office (DEWO) Overview," July 23, 2010. Another Navy briefing: Briefing slide entitled "Surface Navy Laser Vision," in briefing entitled "Navy Directed Energy Efforts – Ship Based Laser Weapon System," July 23, 2010. Industry briefing: Briefing to CRS by an industry firm in the summer of 2010; data shown in table used here with the firm's permission. DSB report: *[Report of] Defense Science Board Task Force on Directed Energy Weapons*, December 2007, Table 2 (page 12). Northrop Grumman research paper: Richard J. Dunn, III, Operational Implications of Laser Weapons, Northrop Grumman (Analysis Center Papers), September 2005 (available online at http://www.northropgrumman.com/analysis-center/paper/assets Operational_Implications_of_La.pdf), visual inspection of Figure 1 (page 7).

Notes: kW is kilowatts; MW is megawatts; km is kilometer; RAM is rockets, artillery, mortars; MANPADS is man-portable air defense system (i.e., shoulder-fired surface-to-air missiles).

a. Note that this statement refers to ground-based operations. It is not clear how this statement might change for shipboard operations, where atmospheric absorption due to water vapor can be an increased concern.

APPENDIX C. NAVY ORGANIZATIONS INVOLVED IN DEVELOPING LASERS

Principal Navy organizations involved in developing lasers for potential shipboard use include

- the Office of Naval Research (ONR);
- the Naval Research Laboratory (NRL);
- the Directed Energy and Electric Weapon Systems (DE&EWS) Program Office (PMS-405);[65]
- the Naval Surface Warfare Center (NSWC) Dahlgren Division (NSWCDD), located at Dahlgren, VA; and
- the Directed Energy Warfare Office (DEWO), which the Navy established in August 2009 to serve as an NSWCDD center of excellence.

Additional Navy organizations involved in developing lasers for potential shipboard use include the CIWS program office (PEO IWS 3B, meaning Program Executive Officer, Integrated Warfare Systems, office code 3B); NSWC Crane Division at Crane, IN; NSWC Port Hueneme at Port Hueneme, CA; the Naval Air Weapon Stations at China Lake and Point Mugu, CA, as well as the Naval Air Station Patuxent River, MD, all of which are part of the Naval Air Systems Command (NAVIAR); and the Space and Naval Warfare Systems (SPARWAR) Center Pacific, located at San Diego.

Additional DOD organizations outside the Navy are also involved in developing lasers for potential shipboard use.

APPENDIX D. ADDITIONAL INFORMATION ON LASER WEAPON SYSTEM (LaWS)

A fiber SSL uses light-emitting diodes (LEDs) to convert electricity into light. The light is then intensified by passing it through one or more flexible optic fibers made of a synthetic crystalline material. The material typically is Nd:YAG—yttrium-aluminum-garnet (YAG) that has been "doped" (i.e., made impure) through the addition of neodymium (Nd). The fibers are referred to as the gain medium, and the laser is called a solid state laser because the gain medium is a solid rather than a liquid (such as in dye lasers) or a gas (as in gas lasers). Over the last decade, dramatic improvements in diodes and fiber materials have enabled a roughly 100-fold increase in the maximum power of an individual fiber SSL, from about 100 watts to about 10 kW.

The Navy's approach to developing LaWS is to maximize reliance on existing technology and components so as to minimize development and procurement costs. The LaWS prototype incoherently combines light beams from six fiber SSLs—commercial, off-the-shelf (COTS) welding lasers—each with a power of 5.5 kW, to create a laser with a total power of 33 kW[66] and a BQ of 17. The light from the six lasers is said to be incoherently combined because the individual beams are not merged into a true single beam (i.e., the individual beams are not brought in phase with each other). Although the beams are quite close to one another, they remain separate and out of phase with each other, and are steered and focused by the beam director so that they converge into a single spot when they reach the intended target. Coherently combining the six beams into a true single beam (i.e., one in which the six beams are "phase locked") would require a system with more-complex internal optics and electronic control systems.

LaWS, like many other fiber SSLs, emits light with a wavelength of 1.064 microns, which is close to, but not exactly at, an atmospheric transmission "sweet spot" at 1.045 microns.

LaWS is about 25% efficient, meaning that about 400 kW of ship's power would be needed to operate a future version of LaWS producing 100 kW of laser light. The remaining 300 kW of electrical energy would be converted into waste thermal energy (heat) that needs to be removed from the system using the ship's cooling capacity.

The conceptual breakthrough underpinning LaWS was made by scientists at the Pennsylvania State Electronic-Optic Center in 2004 and 2005 during some simple experiments, and by scientists at the Naval Research Laboratory (NRL) in 2006, in detailed analysis and subsequent experiments. Both groups showed that coherently combining light beams was not necessary to create a militarily useful laser from commercial fiber SSLs—that this could be done through the technically simpler approach of incoherently combining their beams.

DEWO is the lead system integrator (LSI) and technical direction agent for LaWS. Raytheon, the maker of CIWS, is the prime support contractor for the CIWS integration effort.[67]

Table D-1 shows funding for the LaWS development effort. The Administration's FY2011 budget requested no funding for the LaWS development effort.

Table D-1. Funding for LaWS Development
Millions of dollars, rounded to nearest tenth; totals may not add due to rounding

Fiscal Year	PE 0602890F	PE 0603924F	PE 0135197A	PE 0603563N	PE 0604707N	PE 0604756N	PE 0603925N	Total
2007	0.2	0	0	0	0	0	10.8	11.0
2008	0	0	1.0	0.2	0	0	0.7	1.9
2009	0	0	0	0.3	0.8	2.2	1.2	4.4
2010	0	0.3	0	0	0.8	1.0	8.2	10.2
2011 (requested)	0	0	0	0	0	0	0	0

Source: Navy information paper dated November 12, 2010, on funding history for LaWs, provided to CRS by Navy Office of Legislative Affairs, November 15, 2010.

Notes: PE is Program Element—a line item in a DOD appropriations account. The letter F indicates that the PE is in an Air Force account; the letter A indicates that the PE is in an Army account.; the letter N indicates that the PE is in a Navy account. PE 0135197A is a line item in the Army's operations and maintenance account; the other PEs are line items in the Air Force's research and development account and the Navy's research and development account. PE 0602890F is High Energy Laser Research; PE 0603924F is High Energy Laser Advanced Technology Program; PE 0603563N is Ship Concept Advanced Design; PE 0604707N is Space & Electronic Warfare (SEW) Architecture/Engineering Support; PE 0604756N is Ship Self Defense (Engage: Hard Kill); PE 0603925N is Directed Energy and Electric Weapon System.

Figure D-1 shows a picture of the LaWS prototype; **Figure D-2** shows a rendering of LaWS when installed as an addition to a CIWS mount. In **Figure D-2**, the red-colored tube hanging off the left side of the CIWS mount is the LaWS beam director, and the white device bolted to the right side of the CIWS radome is another LaWS component.

Source: Photograph provided by Navy Office of Legislative Affairs, November 3, 2010.

Figure D-1. Photograph of LaWS Prototype.

Navy Shipboard Lasers for Surface, Air, and Missile Defense... 37

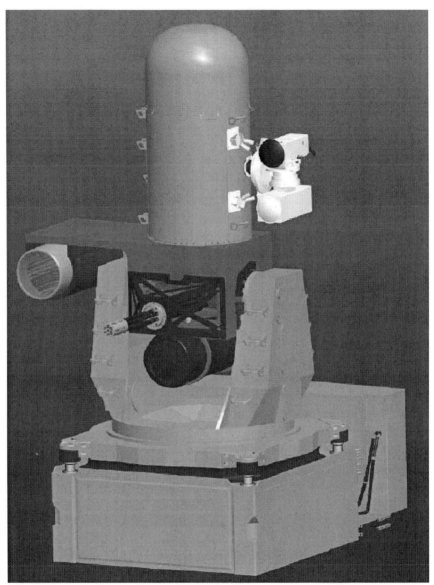

Source: Rendering provided by Navy Office of Legislative Affairs, November 3, 2010. In this rendering, the redcolored tube hanging off the left side of the CIWS mount is the LaWS beam director, and the white device bolted to the right side of the CIWS radome is another LaWS component.

Figure D-2. Rendering of LaWS Integrated on CIWS Mount.

APPENDIX E. ADDITIONAL INFORMATION ON MARITIME LASER DEMONSTRATION (MLD)

Slab SSLs are similar to fiber SSLs, except that the synthetic crystalline material used as the gain medium is formed into plate-like slabs rather than flexible fibers. Slab SSLs are being developed not just by the Navy, but by other U.S. military services, permitting the Navy to leverage development work funded by other parts of DOD.

MLD coherently combines beams from multiple slab SSLs, each with a power of 15 kW, to create a higher-power beam with a good BQ. Each 15 kW laser is housed in a Line Replaceable Unit (LRU) measuring about 1 foot by 2 feet by 3.5 feet. MLD might be installed on its own mount rather than as an addition to a ship's existing CIWS mount.

MLD, like LaWS, emits light with a wavelength of 1.064 microns, which is close to, but not exactly at, an atmospheric transmission "sweet spot" at 1.045 microns.

Slab SSLs are currently about 20% to 25% efficient, meaning that about 400 kW to 500 kW of a ship's power would be needed to operate a system producing 100 kW of laser light. The remaining 300 kW to 400 kW of electrical energy would be converted into waste thermal energy that needs to be removed from the system using the ship's cooling capacity. Future slab SSLs might have efficiencies of about 30%.

In March 2009, Northrop demonstrated a version of MLD that coherently combined seven slab SSLs, each with a power of about 15 kW, to create a beam with a power of about 105 kW and a BQ of less than 3.[68]

Scaling up a slab laser to a total power of 300 kW and a BQ of 2 is not considered to require any technological breakthroughs. A slab laser with a total power of 300 kW might require a below-deck space measuring roughly 4.5 feet by 8 feet by 12 feet. Supporters of slab SSLs such as MLD believe they could eventually be scaled up further, to perhaps 600 kW. Slab SSLs are not generally viewed as easily scalable to megawatt power levels.

MLD is a commercially integrated weapon system with Northrop and L3-Brashears as the principal contractors. The government test team includes NSWC Dahlgren (VA), NSWC Port Hueneme (CA), and NAWC China Lake (CA). Although Northrop is the primary contractor for MLD, several other firms, such as Raytheon and Textron, are involved in efforts to develop slab SSLs for potential use by U.S. military services.

Table E-1 shows Navy funding for the MLD development effort.

Navy Shipboard Lasers for Surface, Air, and Missile Defense... 39

Table E-1. Funding for MLD Development
Millions of dollars, rounded to nearest tenth;
totals may not add due to rounding

Fiscal Year	PE 0602114N	PE 0603114N	PE 0603758N	TOTAL
2008	0	3.2	0	3.2
2009	0.2	0	1.4	1.6
2010	4.0	0	3.1	7.2
2011 (requested)	0	0	0	0

Source: ONR briefing to CRS, July 23, 2010.

Notes: PE is Program Element—a line item in a DOD research and development account. The letter N indicates that the PE is in the Navy's research and development account. PE 0602114N is Power Projection Applied Research; PE 0603114N is Power Projection Advanced Technology; PE 0603758N is Navy Warfighting Experiments and Demonstrations.

Figure E-1 shows the MLD on a trailer; **Figure E-2** shows a schematic of the system; **Figure E-3** shows a rendering of the beam director for the MLD in a notional shipboard installation.

Source: Photograph provided by Navy, November 29, 2010.

Figure E-1. Photograph of MLD on Trailer.

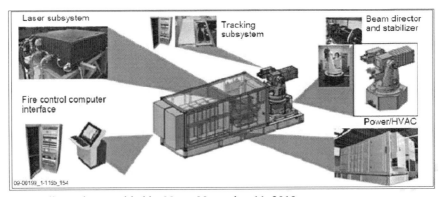

Source: Illustration provided by Navy, November 11, 2010.

Figure E-2. Schematic of MLD.

Source: Photograph provided by Northrop, October 21, 2010.

Figure E-3. Rendering of MLD in Notional Shipboard Installation.

APPENDIX F. ADDITIONAL INFORMATION ON FREE ELECTRON LASER (FEL)

An FEL uses an electron gun to generate a stream of electrons. The electrons are then sent into a linear particle accelerator to accelerate them to light speeds. The accelerated electrons are then sent into a device, known informally as a wiggler, that exposes the electrons to a transverse magnetic field, which causes the electrons to "wiggle" from side to side and release some of their energy in the form of light (photons). The photons are then bounced between mirrors and emitted as a coherent beam of laser light. To increase the efficiency of the system, some of the electrons are then cycled back to the front of the particle accelerator via an energy recovery loop.[69]

Unlike an SSL, which emits light with a fixed wavelength determined by the composition of its gain medium, an FEL's components can be adjusted to change the wavelength of light that it emits, so as to match various atmospheric transmission "sweet spots." The basic architecture of an FEL offers a clear potential for scaling up to power levels of one or more megawatts. A well-designed FEL can in theory be increased in power from 10 kW to 1 MW without an increase in system size, and without need for beam combiners. An FEL emits a beam with a BQ of 1 or close to 1.

Schematics of notional or developmental shipboard FELs today generally show them as devices with a length of roughly 100 feet. An FEL's ultimate shipboard space requirements will depend in part on how it is integrated into a ship's design, and whether the FEL uses room-temperature or superconducting particle-acceleration structures. Using superconducting acceleration structures can reduce the length of an FEL, and would require the use of cryogenic equipment to bring the superconducting structures down to the very low temperatures needed to make them superconducting. Operating an FEL would result in the production of X rays, requiring the system to be shielded to protect the ship's crew and other parts of the ship.

FELs that recycle electrons have an efficiency of about 10%, meaning that about 10 MW of ship's power would be needed to operate an FEL producing 1 MW of laser light. The remaining 900 kW of electrical energy is converted into waste thermal energy.

The FEL development effort is led by ONR. The effort also includes several other Navy organizations and institutions,[70] four Department of Energy (DOE) laboratories,[71] and several universities.[72] Contractors involved in FEL development have included Boeing (CA), Raytheon (MA), SAIC (VA),

Niowave (MI), and Advanced Energy Systems (NY). Boeing and Raytheon competed for the contract to design the 100 kW FEL. In September 2010, ONR announced that it had selected Boeing.[73] The award makes Boeing the Navy's current primary contractor for FEL development.

Table F-1 shows funding for the FEL development effort.

Table F-1. Funding for FEL Development Millions of dollars, rounded to nearest tenth; totals may not add due to rounding

	ONR Core FEL Investment				
Fiscal year	PE 0601153N (directed energy basic science and research)	PE 0602114N (directed energy basic science and research)	PE 0602114N (FEL Innovative Naval Prototype)	Congressional additions[a]	TOTAL
1996	0	0	0	8.6	8.6
1997	0	0	0	5.7	5.7
1998	0	0.2	0	0	0.2
1999	0	0.5	0	0	0.5
2000	0	0.2	0	9.3	9.5
2001	0	0	0	5.0	5.0
2002	0	1.5	0	0	1.5
2003	0	2.4	0	0	2.4
2004	0	9.1	0	6.7	15.8
2005	0	9.0	0	2.0	11.0
2006	1.3	10.1	0	7.0	18.3
2007	1.3	9.1	0	3.5	13.8
2008	1.3	9.3	7.5	2.0	20.2
2009	1.8	8.7	12.8	2.4	25.7
2010	1.9	4.6	18.4	0	24.9
2011 (requested)	2.1	5.1	35.4		42.6

Source: ONR briefing to CRS, July 23, 2010.

Notes: PE is Program Element—a line item in a DOD research and development account. The letter N indicates that the PE is in the Navy's research and development account. PE 0601153N is Defense Research Sciences; PE 0602114N is Power Projection Applied Research.

a. The funding table provided by ONR included a separate data line for congressional additions to requested funding. The additions include funding in the following PEs: 0602111N, 0602270N, 0602114N, 0603114N.

Figure F-1 shows part of an FEL facility at the Thomas Jefferson National Laboratory (Jefferson Lab) in Virginia. Figure F-2 shows a simplified diagram of how an FEL works. Figure F-3 shows a Jefferson Lab schematic of an FEL equipped with two "wigglers"—one for producing infrared (IR) laser light, and one for producing ultraviolet (UV) laser light. The FEL being developed by the Navy for shipboard use would likely produce only infrared light.

Source: Jefferson Lab news release of July 30, 2004, entitled "FEL Achieves 10 Kilowatts," accessed November 16, 2010 at http://www.jlab.org/news/releases/2004/0410kw.html. The news release says that the release is "As released by the Office of Naval Research with images and captions from Jefferson Lab." The caption to the photo in the news release states: "The Free-Electron Laser vault at Jefferson Lab showing the superconducting accelerator in the background and the magnetic wiggler in the foreground. The wiggler converts the electron beam power into laser light. Photo by Greg Adams, JLab."

Figure F-1. Photograph of an FEL Facility.

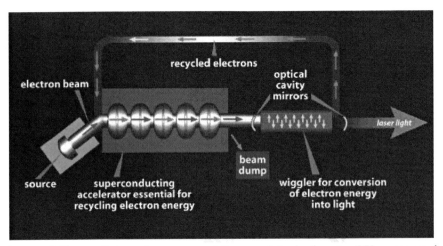

Source: Jefferson Lab web page providing an introduction to FELs, accessed November 16, 2010, at http://www.jlab.org/FEL/feldescrip.html.

Figure F-2. Simplified Diagram of How an FEL Works.

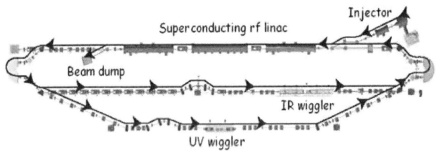

Source: Jefferson Lab web page describing its FEL, accessed November 16, 2010 at http://www.jlab.org/FEL/felspecs.html. This FEL has two "wigglers"—one for producing infrared (IR) laser light, and one for producing ultraviolet (UV) laser light. The FEL being developed by the Navy for shipboard use would likely produce only infrared light. The arrows show the flow of electrons in the device, starting with the electron gun and injector in the upper-right corner. "Rf linac" means radio frequency linear accelerator.

Figure F-3. Schematic of an FEL. (Version with two "wigglers").

APPENDIX G. INNOVATIVE NAVAL PROTOTYPES (INPS)

The Office of Naval Researach (ONR) is developing the 100 kW FEL as an Innovative Naval Prototype (INP). ONR describes INPs as follows:

> [ONR's work on] Leap Ahead Innovations include Innovative Naval Prototypes (INPs) and Swampworks, and are technology investments that are potentially "game changing" or "disruptive" in nature. INPs achieve a level of technology suitable for transition in four to eight years. Innovative Naval Prototypes explore high 6.2 and 6.3 [research and development budget category] technologies that can dramatically change the way Naval forces fight. Programs in this category may be disruptive technologies that, for reasons of high risk or radical departure from established requirements and concepts of operation, are unlikely to survive without top leadership endorsement, and, unlike Future Naval Capabilities [another category of ONR's work], are initially too high risk for a firm transition commitment from the acquisition community. INPs should be identified based on a balanced combination of naval need and technology exploitation. Investments should be planned with the critical mass needed to achieve a level of technology maturity suitable for transition in four to eight years. Program Managers (PMs) are primarily selected from ONR, and in order to help facilitate the transition to the acquisition community, Deputy PMs are typically chosen from the Acquisition community. The CNR [Chief of Naval Research], in consultation with senior Navy and Marine Corps leadership, identifies candidate INPs that are then forwarded to Naval S&T [Science and Technology] Corporate Board (ASN-RDA, VCNO and the ACMC) [the Assistant Secretary of the Navy, Research, Development, and Acquisition, the Vice Chief of Naval Operations, and the Assistant Commandant of the Marine Corps] for approval / disapproval. Free Electron Laser is an innovative naval prototype. Swampworks efforts are smaller in scope than INPs and are intended to produce results in one to three years. This category is where we typically accept higher risk in an effort to produce higher payoff for the warfighters.[74]

APPENDIX H. DOD TECHNOLOGY READINESS LEVELS (TRLS)

DOD uses TRLs to characterize the developmental status of many weapon technologies. DOD defines its TRLs as follows:

- TRL 1: Basic principles observed and reported.

- TRL 2: Technology concept and/or application formulated.
- TRL 3: Analytical and experimental critical function and/or characteristic proof of concept.
- TRL 4: Component and/or breadboard validation in a laboratory environment.
- TRL 5: Component and/or breadboard validation in a relevant environment.
- TRL 6: System/subsystem model or prototype demonstration in a relevant environment.
- TRL 7: System prototype demonstration in an operational environment.
- TRL 8: Actual system completed and qualified through test and demonstration.
- TRL 9: Actual system proven through successful mission operations.[75]

APPENDIX I. PROTOCOL ON BLINDING LASERS

This appendix provides information on the international protocol on blinding lasers and its relationship to DOD laser programs, including the lasers discussed in this report.

Overview

The United States in 1995 ratified the 1980 Convention on Prohibitions or Restriction on the Use of Certain Conventional Weapons Which May be Deemed to be Excessively Injurious or to Have Indiscriminate Effects. An international review of the convention began in 1994 and concluded in May 1996 with the adoption of, among other things, a new Protocol IV on blinding laser weapons. The protocol prohibits the employment of lasers that are specifically designed to cause permanent blindness to the naked eye or to the eye with corrective eyesight devices.

Although the United States has not ratified this protocol, DOD views the protocol as fully consistent with DOD policy. DOD believes the lasers discussed in this report are consistent with DOD policy of prohibiting the use of lasers specifically designed to cause permanent blindness to the naked eye or to the eye with corrective eyesight devices.

Article-by-Article Discussion

Article 1 of the protocol prohibits the employment of "laser weapons specifically designed, as their sole combat function or as one of their combat functions, to cause permanent blindness to unenhanced vision, that is to the naked eye or to the eye with corrective eyesight devices." DOD states that:

> This prohibition is fully consistent with the policy of the Department of Defense, which is to prohibit the use of weapons so designed. Although the prospect of mass blinding was an impetus for the adoption of the Protocol, it was not the intent of the Conference to prohibit only mass blinding. Accordingly, under both the Blinding Laser Protocol and Department of Defense policy, laser weapons designed specifically to cause such permanent blindness may not be used against an individual enemy combatant.[76]

Article 2 of the protocol obligates parties to "take all feasible precautions to avoid the incidence of permanent blindness to unenhanced vision." DOD states that "This requirement is also fully consistent with the policy of the Department of Defense which is to reduce, through training and doctrine, inadvertent injuries from the use of lasers designed for other purposes, such as range-finding, target discrimination, and communications."[77]

Article 3 of the protocol states that "blinding as an incidental or collateral effect of the legitimate military employment of laser systems, including laser systems used against optical equipment, is not covered" by the Protocol. DOD states that this article "reflects a recognition of the inevitability of eye injury as the result of lawful battlefield laser use. Its use is an important measure in avoiding war crimes allegations where injury occurs from legitimate laser uses."[78]

DOD further states that

> As a matter of policy, the United States will refrain from the use of laser weapons prohibited by the Protocol. Therefore, while the Blinding Laser Weapons Protocol does not legally apply to all armed conflicts, it is U.S. policy to apply the Protocol to all such conflicts, however they may be characterized, and in peacetime.... The Protocol is fully consistent with U.S. military interests, Department of Defense policy and humanitarian concerns generally. Accordingly, the United States should ratify it at an early date.[79]

Excerpt from 2007 DSB Task Force Report

A 2007 report by a Defense Science Board (DSB) task force on directed energy weapons stated:

> The task force heard concerns over the legal and policy aspects of employing directed energy weapons. The concern is seen by some as inhibiting or deterring development of such weapons with [i.e., due to] reluctance to invest in capabilities that might not be useable in the battlespace due to legal or policy constraints. Much of this concern is the product of inadequate communications rather than any unusual legal or policy constraints.
>
> The Office of the Secretary of Defense and service component Judge Advocate General Offices have determined that directed energy weapons are, in and of themselves, legal according to all U.S. laws, [as well as] the [international] Laws of Armed Conflict, and are consistent with all current U.S. treaty and international obligations. Noting that directed energy weapons are legal does not imply that their use in a particular situation is legal. There are situations where the use of a directed energy weapon could be contrary to U.S. or international law. This consideration is the case with virtually any weapon.

One such constraint is the use of a laser weapon to intentionally blind combatants. The States Parties to the 1980 Convention on Prohibitions or Restrictions on the use of Certain Conventional Weapons Which May Be Deemed to be Excessively Injurious or to have Indiscriminate Effects had a fourth protocol adopted in 1995, where the intent is to prohibit laser weapons that are specifically used to blind combatants systematically and intentionally. While the United States is not a signatory to this particular protocol, the DOD has issued a policy that prohibits the use of lasers specifically designed to cause permanent blindness of unenhanced vision.

> That same policy stated that "... laser systems are absolutely vital to our modern military. Among other things, they are currently used for detection, targeting, range-finding, communications, and target destruction. They provide a critical technological edge to U.S. forces and allow our forces to fight, win, and survive on an increasingly lethal battlefield. In addition, lasers provide significant humanitarian benefits. They allow weapon systems to be increasingly discriminate, thereby reducing collateral damage to civilian lives and property. The [DOD] recognizes that accidental or incidental eye injuries may occur on the battlefield as the result of the use of legitimate laser systems.[80] Therefore,

we continue to strive, through training and doctrine, to minimize these injuries."

A similarly supportive policy has been stated for other directed energy weapons. At the same time, when such weapons are new to the battlespace, there will be a policy determination on their initial introduction to include an understanding by appropriate policy makers of the intended uses. Such determination needs to be informed by a thorough and credible understanding of the risk and benefits of employing such weapons. Beyond the process of approving first use, the expectation is that the Laws of Armed Conflict, rules of engagement, and combat commander direction will govern employment of directed energy weapons as is the case for kinetic weapons.[81]

APPENDIX J. ILLUMINATION OF OBJECTS IN SPACE

In briefings on potential shipboard lasers, Navy officials noted DOD Instruction (DODI) 3100.11 of March 31, 2000, which states in part:

> All DoD laser activities shall be conducted in a safe and responsible manner that protects space systems, their mission effectiveness, and humans in space, consistent with national security requirements, in accordance with [DoD Directive 3100.10, "Space Policy," July 9, 1999]. All such activities shall be coordinated with the Commander in Chief of U.S. Space Command (CINCSPACE) for predictive avoidance or deconfliction with U.S., friendly, and other space operations.[82]

The technical community in the Navy believes that this instruction effectively requires the military services to implement measures for ensuring that objects in space face low or no exposure to laser energy. The technical community believes that this in turn would require that shipboard lasers incorporate so-called predictive avoidance (PA) software and/or other features that would prevent them from firing in the direction of an object in space. The community believes that two policy changes would be required to permit Navy surface ships to use shipboard lasers with power levels high enough that they could cause unwanted collateral damage to satellites:

- The community believes that current safety criteria relating to satellites are overly restrictive and should be replaced with a new policy that includes what the Navy views as more realistic safety criteria.

- The community believes that certain data relating to sensitive satellites should be removed from the PA system so that the classification level of the PA system can be lowered.

APPENDIX K. SECTION 220 OF FY2000 DEFENSE AUTHORIZATION ACT (P.L. 106-398)

As mentioned earlier (see "Options for Congress"), the option of directing the Navy to develop and install lasers with certain capabilities on a certain number of Navy surface ships by a certain date could take the form of a provision broadly similar to Section 220 of the FY2001 defense authorization act (H.R. 4205/P.L. 106-398 of October 30, 2000), which set goals for the deployment of unmanned combat aircraft and unmanned combat vehicles. The text of Section 220 is as follows:

> SEC. 220. UNMANNED ADVANCED CAPABILITY COMBAT AIRCRAFT AND GROUND COMBAT VEHICLES.
> (a) GOAL- It shall be a goal of the Armed Forces to achieve the fielding of unmanned, remotely controlled technology such that—
> (1) by 2010, one-third of the aircraft in the operational deep strike force aircraft fleet are unmanned; and
> (2) by 2015, one-third of the operational ground combat vehicles are unmanned.
> (b) REPORT ON UNMANNED ADVANCED CAPABILITY COMBAT AIRCRAFT AND GROUND COMBAT VEHICLES- (1) Not later than January 31, 2001, the Secretary of Defense shall submit to the congressional defense committees a report on the programs to demonstrate unmanned advanced capability combat aircraft and ground combat vehicles undertaken jointly between the Director of the Defense Advanced Research Projects Agency and any of the following:
> (A) The Secretary of the Army.
> (B) The Secretary of the Navy.
> (c) The Secretary of the Air Force.
> (2) The report shall include, for each program referred to in paragraph (1), the following:
> (A) A schedule for the demonstration to be carried out under that program.
> (B) An identification of the funding required for fiscal year 2002 and for the future-years defense program to carry out that program and for the demonstration to be carried out under that program.

(C) In the case of the program relating to the Army, the plan for modification of the existing memorandum of agreement with the Defense Advanced Research Projects Agency for demonstration and development of the Future Combat System to reflect an increase in unmanned, remotely controlled enabling technologies.

(3) The report shall also include, for each Secretary referred to in paragraphs (1)(A), (1)(B), and (1)(C), a description and assessment of the acquisition strategy for unmanned advanced capability combat aircraft and ground combat vehicles planned by that Secretary, which shall include a detailed estimate of all research and development, procurement, operation, support, ownership, and other costs required to carry out such strategy through the year 2030, and—

(A) in the case of the acquisition strategy relating to the Army, the transition from the planned acquisition strategy for the Future Combat System to an acquisition strategy capable of meeting the goal specified in subsection (a)(2);

(B) in the case of the acquisition strategy relating to the Navy—

(i) the plan to implement a program that examines the ongoing Air Force unmanned combat air vehicle program and identifies an approach to develop a Navy unmanned combat air vehicle program that has the goal of developing an aircraft that is suitable for aircraft carrier use and has maximum commonality with the aircraft under the Air Force program; and

(ii) an analysis of alternatives between the operational deep strike force aircraft fleet and that fleet together with an additional 10 to 20 unmanned advanced capability combat aircraft that are suitable for aircraft carrier use and capable of penetrating fully operational enemy air defense systems; and

(C) in the case of the acquisition strategy relating to the Air Force—

(i) the schedule for evaluation of demonstration results for the ongoing unmanned combat air vehicle program and the earliest possible transition of that program into engineering and manufacturing development and procurement; and

(ii) an analysis of alternatives between the currently planned deep strike force aircraft fleet and the operational deep strike force aircraft fleet that could be acquired by fiscal year 2010 to meet the goal specified in subsection (a)(1).

(iii) FUNDS- Of the amount authorized to be appropriated for Defense-wide activities under section 201(4) for the Defense Advanced Research Projects Agency, $100,000,000 shall be available only to carry out the programs referred to in subsection (b)(1).

(d) DEFINITIONS- For purposes of this section:

(1) An aircraft or ground combat vehicle has 'unmanned advanced capability' if it is an autonomous, semi-autonomous, or remotely controlled system that can be deployed, re-tasked, recovered, and re-deployed.

(2) The term 'currently planned deep strike force aircraft fleet' means the early entry, deep strike aircraft fleet (composed of F-117 stealth aircraft and B-2 stealth aircraft) that is currently planned for fiscal year 2010.

(3) The term 'operational deep strike force aircraft fleet' means the currently planned deep strike force aircraft fleet, together with at least 30 unmanned advanced capability combat aircraft that are capable of penetrating fully operational enemy air defense systems.

(4) The term 'operational ground combat vehicles' means ground combat vehicles acquired through the Future Combat System acquisition program of the Army to equip the future objective force, as outlined in the vision statement of the Chief of Staff of the Army.

End Notes

[1] For more on China's ASBM development effort, see CRS Report RL33153, China Naval Modernization: Implications for U.S. Navy Capabilities—Background and Issues for Congress, by Ronald O'Rourke.

[2] This appears to be a reference to the November 2010 test of the Maritime Laser Demonstration (MLD) system discussed later in this report.

[3] Grace V. Jean, "Navy Aiming for Laser Weapons at Sea," National Defense, August 2010, accessed online at http://www.nationaldefensemagazine.org/archive/2010/August/Pages/NavyAimingforLaserWeaponsatSea.aspx.

[4] A program of record, or POR, is a term sometimes used by DOD officials that means, in general, a program in the Future Years Defense Plan (FYDP) that is intended to provide a new, improved, or continuing materiel, weapon, or information system or service capability in response to an approved need. The term is sometimes used to refer to a program in a service's budget for procuring and deploying an operational weapon system, as opposed to a research and development effort that might or might not eventually lead to procurement and deployment of an operational weapon system. If a research and development effort is converted into a program or record for procuring an operational weapon system, the program might then be conducted under the DOD's process for managing the acquisition of weapon systems, which is discussed further in CRS Report RL34026, Defense Acquisitions: How DOD Acquires Weapon Systems and Recent Efforts to Reform the Process, by Moshe Schwartz.

[5] The RAND briefing was based on an evaluation of directed energy technologies that RAND performed for the Navy. At the Navy's direction, RAND collaborated on the study with the Center for Naval Analysis (CNA) and the MITRE Corporation.

[6] In discussions of other types of defense systems, the terms short range and long range could have considerably different meanings. In discussions of the ranges of military airplanes or

ballistic missiles, for example, the term short range might mean a range of hundreds of miles, while references to longer ranges could refer to ranges of thousands of miles.

[7] See, for example, Geoff Fein, "Navy Leveraging Commercial Lasers To Shoot Down UAVs," Defense Daily, May 11, 2010: 3-4.

[8] The Navy's short-range shipboard interceptor missiles include Rolling Airframe Missiles (RAMs), which currently have a unit procurement cost (including canisters and other associated hardware) of about $800,000, and Evolved Sea Sparrow Missiles (ESSMs), which currently have a unit procurement cost (including canisters and other associated hardware) of about $1.4 million. The Navy's longer-range interceptor is the Standard Missile (SM). Air defense versions of the Standard Missile currently have a unit procurement cost (including containers and other associated hardware) of about $4.3 million. (Source: Navy budget-justification book for Weapon Procurement, Navy [WPN] appropriation account for FY2011.) As discussed in another CRS report (CRS Report RL33745, Navy Aegis Ballistic Missile Defense (BMD) Program: Background and Issues for Congress, by Ronald O'Rourke), ballistic missile defense versions of the Standard Missile have unit procurement costs of $9 million to $15 million.

[9] A "hard kill" involves destroying the attacking weapon in some manner. A "soft kill" involves confusing the weapon through decoys or other measures, so that it misses its intended target.

[10] Reversible jamming means that the jamming does not damage the sensor, and that the sensor can resume normal operations once the jamming ends.

[11] An aerostat is a lighter-than-air object, such as a dirigible or balloon, that can stay stationary in the air.

[12] For further discussion, see P. Sprangle, J.R. Peñano, A. Ting, and B. Hafizi, "Propagation of High-Energy Lasers in a Maritime Atmosphere," NRL Review 2004. (Accessed online at http://www.nrl.navy.mil/research/nrl-review/2004/ featured-research/sprangle/.)

[13] Lasers being developed for potential shipboard use produce light with wavelengths in the near-infrared portion of the spectrum. Sweet spots in this part of the spectrum include wavelengths of 0.87 microns, 1.045 microns, 1.24 microns, 1.62 microns, 2.13 microns, and 2.2 microns. (Other sources, such as the research paper cited in footnote 12, cite somewhat different figures for sweet spot wavelengths, depending in part on whether sweet spot is for water vapor alone, or for multiple sources of atmospheric absorption and scattering.)

[14] The Navy installs multiple CIWS systems on certain ships not only to improve their ability to handle a saturation attack, but also to ensure that each ship has full (i.e., 360-degree CIWS) coverage around the ship. A desire for 360- degree laser coverage could be another reason for installing multiple lasers on a ship.

[15] For a discussion of laser power levels, see "Required Laser Power Levels for Countering Targets".

[16] For more on the issue of collateral damage to satellites, see Appendix J.

[17] For an additional (and somewhat similar) discussion of the potential advantages and limitations of lasers, see Richard J. Dunn, III, Operational Implications of Laser Weapons, Northrop Grumman Analysis Center Papers, September 2005, pp. 10-12.

[18] Swarm boats are small, fast boats that attack a larger ship by operating in packs, or swarms, so as to present the larger ship with a complex situation of many hostile platforms that are moving rapidly around the ship in different directions.

[19] A laser with perfect BQ – meaning that the laser's light spot is focused to the physical diffraction limit – is said to have a BQ of 1.0. A beam that is focused to the physical diffraction limit is focused as well as the laws of nature allow. Lasers with the wavelengths

considered in this report that are focused to the physical diffraction limit would, if fired in a vacuum, experience very little spreading out of the laser spot as the beam travels further and further from the source. A BQ of 2.0 means that the laser's light spot at a given range is twice as large in diameter as an otherwise-same laser with a BQ of 1. The Navy considers a BQ of 1.1 to 5 to be high, and a BQ of 5.1 to 20 to be moderate. Achieving a BQ of 1 to 5 generally adds complexity and cost to the system. In general, the longer the range to the target, the more important BQ becomes.

[20] As discussed earlier, atmospheric absorption, scattering, and turbulence are affected by the laser's light wavelength and the use of adaptive optics.

[21] Jitter becomes more important as BQ improves and range increases.

[22] Some military lasers, such as the Air Force's Airborne laser (ABL), are chemically powered. Development work on potential shipboard lasers focuses on electrically powered lasers because such lasers can be powered by a ship's existing electrical power system, whereas a chemically powered laser would require the ship to be periodically resupplied with the chemicals used by the laser. Resupplying the ship with the chemicals could require the ship to temporarily remove itself from the battle. In addition, the Navy would need to establish a new logistics train to provide the chemicals to Navy surface ships, and loading and storing the chemicals on ships would create a handling risk for crew members, since the chemicals in question are toxic.

[23] As mentioned earlier the Phalanx CIWS is a radar-controlled Gatling gun that fires bursts of 20mm shells.

[24] Threat-representative means that the UAV is generally similar in design and capabilities to UAVs operated by potential adversaries.

[25] For a Navy press release about this test, see NAVSEA (Naval Sea Systems Command) press release dated May 28, 2010, and entitled "Navy Laser Destroys Unmanned Aerial Vehicle in a Maritime Environment," accessed online at http://www.navsea.navy.mil/PR2010/ PressRelease_20100528_Laser%20Destroys%20UAV.pdf. The UAVs engaged in these tests were BQM-147s, which various sources describe as low-cost, propeller-driven UAVs with a length of about 5 feet, a wingspan of about 8 feet, and a maximum speed of 100 knots or less.

[26] Source: Navy information paper dated December 3, 2010, provided by the Navy to CRS on December 3, 2010. DOD uses TRL ratings to characterize the developmental status of many weapon technologies. DOD TRL ratings range from 1 (basic principles observed and reported) to 9 (actual system proven through successful mission operations). For the definitions of all 9 DOD TRL ratings, see Appendix H.

[27] The $17 million figure was provided in a Navy briefing to CRS. A May 11, 2010, press report quoted a Navy official as estimating the cost at $15 million:

"I think the total system, when we finally get it out there, will be on the order of $15 million per system and then there will be no ordnance costs, no logistics tail for maintaining the ordnance, no depots to overhaul ordnance, and no fire suppression as you move this ordnance around," [Capt. Dave Kiel, Naval Sea Systems Command (NAVSEA) directed energy and electric weapons program manager] said.

(Geoff Fein, "Navy Leveraging Commercial Lasers To Shoot Down UAVs," Defense Daily, May 11, 2010: 3-4.)

[28] See Northrop Grumman press release dated July 26, 2010, and entitled "Northrop Grumman-Built Maritime Laser Demonstration System Proves Key Capabilities for Shipboard Operations, Weaponization," accessed online at http://www.irconnect.com/ noc/press/pages/news_releases.html?d=197321.

[29] See Northrop Grumman press release dated September 30, 2010, and entitled "Northrop Grumman-Built Maritime Laser Demonstration System Shows Higher Lethality, Longer Ranges at Potomac River Test Range; U.S. Navy Solid-State Laser's Mature Technology is Ready for Marine Environment;" accessed online at http://www.irconnect.com/noc/press/pages/news_releases.html?d=202703.

[30] Andrew Burt, "Navy's First At-Sea Maritime laser Weapon Test Encounters Delays," Inside the Navy, November 15, 2010.

[31] Source: Navy information paper dated December 3, 2010, provided by the Navy to CRS on December 3, 2010. As mentioned in footnote 26, DOD uses TRL ratings to characterize the developmental status of many weapon technologies. DOD TRL ratings range from 1 (basic principles observed and reported) to 9 (actual system proven through successful mission operations). For the definitions of all 9 DOD TRL ratings, see Appendix H.

[32] For a description of INPs, see Appendix G.

[33] A low power Terahertz Sensor FEL is also being developed under the INP, with a prototype scheduled to be available in FY2015. ONR states that "Possible uses of this system include [target] interrogation, sensing and discrimination of high value targets, and weapons of mass destruction detection."

[34] Source: Navy information paper dated December 3, 2010, provided by the Navy to CRS on December 3, 2010. As mentioned in footnote 26, DOD uses TRL ratings to characterize the developmental status of many weapon technologies. DOD TRL ratings range from 1 (basic principles observed and reported) to 9 (actual system proven through successful mission operations). For the definitions of all 9 DOD TRL ratings, see Appendix H.

[35] The term socialization as used by DOD personnel generally refers to the process in which people learn about and become comfortable with a new idea or technology.

[36] Geoff Fein, "Navy Leveraging Commercial Lasers To Shoot Down UAVs," Defense Daily, May 11, 2010: 3-4.

[37] As mentioned earlier (see footnote 19), BQ is a measure of how well-focused the beam is.

[38] MANPADS stands for man-portable air defense system.

[39] See, for example, Andrew Burt, "Roughead Seeks 'Revolutionary' Concepts In Information and Computing," Inside the Navy, October 11, 2010.

[40] See, for example, Andrew Burt, "Navy Approves Three of 14 Information Dominance Roadmaps," Inside the Navy, September 10, 2010; "Notes from the Armed Forces Communications and Electronics Association and U.S. Naval Institute's West 2010 Conference," Inside the Navy, February 8, 2010.

[41] See, for example, "Navy Roadmap Calls For Spiral Development Of Fire Scout UAV," Inside the Navy, August 2, 2010.

[42] See, for example, Cid Standifer, "Navy To Work With Air Force To Analyze And Exploit Intelligence Data," Inside the Navy, July 30, 2010.

[43] Emelie Rutherford, "Navy To Unveil Master Plan for Unmanned Surface Vehicles This Month," Inside the Navy, September 10, 2007.

[44] For more on the Navy's Arctic roadmap, see CRS Report R41153, Changes in the Arctic: Background and Issues for Congress, coordinated by Ronald O'Rourke.

[45] See, for example, Zachary M. Peterson, "Navy Issues Climate Change Roadmap, Defers Investments Pending Studty," Inside the Navy, May 31, 2010.

[46] See, for example, Randy Woods, "'Naval Transformation Roadmap' Fleshes Out 'Seapower 21' Vision," Inside the Navy, July 8, 2002.

[47] See CRS Report RS21195, Evolutionary Acquisition and Spiral Development in DOD Programs: Policy Issues for Congress, by Gary J. Pagliano and Ronald O'Rourke.

[48] Richard J. Dunn, III, Operational Implications of Laser Weapons, Northrop Grumman Analysis Center Papers, September 2005, p. 9.

[49] Richard J. Dunn, III, Operational Implications of Laser Weapons, Northrop Grumman Analysis Center Papers, September 2005, p. 24. The paper also stated on page 5:

The challenge to the U.S. military is that our understanding of laser weapons technologies is outpacing efforts to bring these capabilities into the force. Available funding for laser weapons development lags behind what would be necessary to bring technologies to maturity as quickly as possible. Equally threatening to the success of laser weapons in the field is the lack of attention to concept development for laser weapons operational employment. This situation is neither new nor unique to laser weapons. Historically, technical development of new warfighting capabilities – everything from ironclad warships, to heavier-than-air aircraft, to tanks, radar and radar-defeating "stealth" – has proceeded faster than military forces can adapt their warfighting approaches to incorporate the full advantage of the new capability.

Unfortunately, this imbalance frequently means that weapons developers move along at great speed in designing advanced systems with tremendous battlefield potential, but they do so in splendid intellectual isolation. Lacking the guiding hand of operational requirements, they are unable to properly prioritize resources or focus on the weapons capabilities that are most important to warfighters. They can waste precious time and resources pursuing weapons capabilities of lesser operational utility while foregoing development of those that might truly provide a decisive advantage. Just as sadly, military forces can field an expensive and promising new capability that remains underutilized because warfighters do not fully understand how to employ it to its greatest advantage. In today's fast-changing threat environment, given tight Defense resources and the exciting possibilities offered by development of laser weapons, the U.S. cannot afford the wasted time or resources of such mistakes in developing one of the next breakthrough technologies.

[50] Cover memorandum dated November 26, 2007, from William Schneider, Jr., DSB Chairman, to the Under Secretary of Defense for Acquisition, Technology, and Logistics, transmitting the final report of the Defense Science Board task force on directed energy weapon systems and technology applications.

[51] Undated cover memorandum from General Larry D. Welch and Dr. Robert J. Hermann, Co-Chairs, to the Chairman, Defense Science Board, transmitting the final report of the Defense Science Board task force on directed energy weapon systems and technology applications.

[52] [Report of] Defense Science Board Task Force on Directed Energy Weapons, Washington, December 2007, pp. ix-x.

[53] [Report of] Defense Science Board Task Force on Directed Energy Weapons, Washington, December 2007, pp. 47-48.

[54] Thomas Ehrhard, Andrew Krepinevich, and Barry Watts, "Near-Term Prospects for Battlefield Directed-Energy Weapons," Washington, Center for Strategic and Budgetary Assessments, January 2009, pp. 3 and 4.

[55] Thomas Ehrhard, Andrew Krepinevich, and Barry Watts, "Near-Term Prospects for Battlefield Directed-Energy Weapons," Washington, Center for Strategic and Budgetary Assessments, January 2009, p. 3.

[56] Free space optics are those arranged so that the light travels from one optical element (such as a mirror) to another, with an air gap (i.e., free space) in between.

[57] LRUs are sealed, box-like containers enclosing many of a weapon's components. LRUs support a modular approach to maintenance in which personnel repair the weapon by removing a faulty LRU and replacing it with another.

[58] For more on the Flight III DDG-51, see CRS Report RL32109, Navy DDG-51 and DDG-1000 Destroyer Programs: Background and Issues for Congress, by Ronald O'Rourke.

[59] Grace V. Jean, "Navy Aiming for Laser Weapons at Sea," National Defense, August 2010, accessed online at http://www.nationaldefensemagazine.org/archive/2010/August/Pages/NavyAimingforLaserWeaponsatSea.aspx.

[60] The issue of thermal blooming in "down-the-throat" engagements is of particular concern for a megawatt-class laser. Since carriers and amphibious assault ships are potential high-value targets for an attacker, it might make more operational sense to install megawatt-class FELs on ships other than carriers or amphibious assault ships, so that those other ships could use their FELs to counter targets that are flying a crossing path toward a carrier or amphibious assault ship.

[61] For more on the CG(X) program, see CRS Report RL34179, Navy CG(X) Cruiser Program: Background for Congress, by Ronald O'Rourke.

[62] For more on the option of a new-design destroyer, see CRS Report RL32109, Navy DDG-51 and DDG-1000 Destroyer Programs: Background and Issues for Congress, by Ronald O'Rourke.

[63] For more on the CVN-78 program, see CRS Report RS20643, Navy Ford (CVN-78) Class Aircraft Carrier Program: Background and Issues for Congress, by Ronald O'Rourke.

[64] This option could take the form of a provision broadly similar to Section 220 of the FY2001 defense authorization act (H.R. 4205/P.L. 106-398 of October 30, 2000), which set goals for the deployment of unmanned combat aircraft and unmanned combat vehicles. For the text of Section 220, see Appendix K.

[65] PMS-405 means Project Manager, Shipbuilding, office code 405.

[66] A June 6, 2010, press report states that "The system uses six commercial off-the-shelf five-and-a-half kilowatt welding lasers...." (Dan Taylor, "Navy Testing Developmental Laser Against Small Surface Vessels," Inside the Navy, June 7, 2010.) Another source puts the total power of LaWS at 32 kW. (Larry Greenemeier, "U.S. Navy Laser Weapon Shoots Down Drones in Test, ScientificAmerican.com, July 19, 2010, accessed online at http://www.scientificamerican.com/article.cfm?id=laser-downs-uavs.)

[67] Other firms involved in the LaWS effort include IPG Photonics (the maker of the fiber SSLs), L-3 Communications, and Boeing. The LaWS effort also involves the Pennsylvania State University Electro-Optics Center and the Johns Hopkins University Applied Physics Laboratory.

[68] See Northrop Grumman press release dated March 18, 2009, and entitled "Northrop Grumman Scales New Heights in Electric Laser Power, Achieves 100 Kilowatts From a Solid-State Laser," accessed online at http://www.irconnect.com/noc/press/pages/news_releases.html?d=161575.

[69] A 2004 media advisory from the Office of Naval research states:
In the FEL, electrons are stripped from their atoms and then whipped up to high energies by a linear accelerator. From there, they are steered into a wiggler—a device that uses an electromagnetic field to shake the electrons, forcing them to release some of their energy in the form of photons. As in a conventional laser, the photons are bounced between two mirrors and then emitted as a coherent beam of light. However, FEL operators can adjust the wavelength of the laser's emitted light by increasing or decreasing the energies of the electrons in the accelerator or the amount of shaking in the wiggler.
(Office of Naval Research media advisory released July 30, 2004, and entitled "Free-Electron Laser Reaches 10 Kilowatts," accessed online at http://www.onr.navy.mil/Media-Center/Press-Releases/2004/Free-Electron-Laser-10-Kilowatts.aspx).

[70] These include the Naval Postgraduate School in California, the U.S. Naval Academy in Maryland, NRL, NSWC Carderock in Maryland, the Naval Air Weapons Center (NAWC) China Lake in California, NSWCDD, PMS405, and the Naval Warfare Systems Center Pacific (SPAWAR) in California.

[71] These are the Thomas Jefferson National Laboratory in Virginia, the Los Alamos National Laboratory in New Mexico, the Brookhaven National Laboratory in New York, and the Argonne National Laboratory in Illinois.

[72] These include the MIT Lincoln Laboratory in Massachusetts, Vanderbuilt University in Tennessee, Colorado State University, the University of California, the University of Wisconsin, Stanford University in California, Yale University in Connecticut, the University of Texas, and the University of Maryland.

[73] See Department of Defense contract announcement No. 804-10, dated September 7, 2010, accessed online at http://www.defense.gov/contracts/contract.aspx?contractid=4361. See also Geoff Fein, "ONR Awards Boeing $23 Million To Finish Free Electron Laser Design," Defense Daily, September 17, 2010: 3-4.

[74] Source: Navy information paper on directed energy dated August 26, 2010.

[75] Source: Department of Defense, Technology Readiness Assessment (TRA) Deskbook, July 2009, accessed online at http://www.dod.mil/ddre/doc/DoD_TRA_July_2009_Read_Version.pdf.

[76] Department of Defense, CCW: Article by Article Analysis of the Protocol on Blinding Laser Weapons, accessed online at http://www.dod.gov/acq/acic/treaties/ccwapl/artbyart_pro4.htm. In January 1997, Secretary of Defense William Perry issued a memorandum regarding DOD policy on blinding lasers which states in its entirety:
The Department of Defense prohibits the use of lasers specifically designed to cause permanent blindness and supports negotiations to prohibit the use of such weapons. However, laser systems are absolutely vital to our modern military. Among other things, they are currently used for detection, targeting, range-finding, communications, and target destruction. They provide a critical technological edge to U.S. forces and allow our forces to fight, win and survive on an increasingly lethal battlefield. In addition, lasers provide significant humanitarian benefits. They allow weapon systems to be increasingly discriminate, thereby reducing collateral damage to civilian lives and property. The Department of Defense recognizes that accidental or incidental eye injuries may occur on the battlefield as the result of the use of lasers not specifically designed to cause permanent blindness. Therefore, we continue to strive, through training and doctrine, to minimize these injuries.
(Memorandum dated January 17, 1997, from Secretary of Defense William J. Perry to the secretaries of the military departments, et al, on DOD policy on blinding lasers, provided to CRS on October 4, 2010, by the Navy Office of Legislative Affairs.)
Paragraph 4.3 of DOD Instruction 3100.11 of March 31, 2000, on the illumination of objects in space by lasers, states: "The use of lasers specifically designed to cause permanent blindness in humans is prohibited, in accordance with [the above-cited January 17, 1997, memorandum from the Secretary of Defense]."

[77] Department of Defense, CCW: Article by Article Analysis of the Protocol on Blinding Laser Weapons, accessed online at http://www.dod.gov/acq/acic/ treaties/ccwapl/artbyart_pro4.htm.

[78] Department of Defense, CCW: Article by Article Analysis of the Protocol on Blinding Laser Weapons, accessed online at http://www.dod.gov/acq/acic/treaties/ ccwapl/artbyart_pro4.htm.

[79] Department of Defense, CCW: Article by Article Analysis of the Protocol on Blinding Laser Weapons, accessed online at http://www.dod.gov/acq/acic/treaties/ ccwapl/artbyart_pro4.htm.

[80] The text of the 1997 Secretary of Defense memorandum quoted in footnote 76 is slightly different at this point. Instead of "legitimate laser systems," the 1997 memorandum uses the phrase "lasers not specifically designed to cause permanent blindness."

[81] [Report of] Defense Science Board Task Force on Directed Energy Weapons, Washington, December 2007, pp. xiixiii. Ellipsis and material in brackets as in original.

[82] Department of Defense Instruction Number 3100.11, March 31, 2000, on Illumination of Objects in Space by lasers, paragraph 4.2.

In: Navy Shipboard Lasers
Editors: R. E. Griffith, G. L. Coughlin   © 2011 Nova Science Publishers, Inc.
ISBN: 978-1-61324-212-4

Chapter 2

SOLID-STATE FIBER LASER[*]

Office of Navy Research

AT A GLANCE

What is it?

- Solid-State Fiber Laser provides Incoherent Fiber Lasers for short asymmetric threat engagement and Coherent Combined Fiber Lasers for long range aircraft self protection.

How Does It Work?

- A "fi ber" laser is a laser in which the active gain medium is an optical fiber doped with rare-earth elements such as erbium, ytterbium, neodymium, dysprosium, praseodymium and thulium. Light is kept in the "core" of the optical fiber by total internal refl ection. T is causes the fiber to act as a waveguide. Fibers that support many propagation paths or transverse modes are called multi-mode fibers (MMF). Fibers that support only a single mode are called single

---

[*] This is an edited, reformatted and augmented version of an Office of Navy Research publication, dated August 2008.

mode fibers (SMF). MMFs generally have a large-diameter core, and are used for short-distance communication links or for applications where high power must be transmitted. Single mode fibers are used for most communication links longer than 200 meters.

What Will It Accomplish?

- The improved efficiency, reduction in weight, volume, prime power, etc., defines a fiber laser as the best pathway to provide Naval aviation / Navy a 100 kW laser weapon.

The Navy's future fiber laser weapon system is being designed to be game changing and fit into aircraft pods.

The capability of having speedof-light delivery for a wide range of missions and threats is a key element of a future aircraft layered defense.

Understanding the physics for modeling and simulation is necessary for effective testing of smaller and lighter high power solid state lasers.

This technology is scalable, has high optical quality and has a highly compact modular design for high efficiency.

This revolutionary technology allows for multiple payoffs for Naval aviation. The ability for aircraft self protection, time critical strike, precision engagements, graduated lethality, low collateral damage, and asymmetric threat engagement allow for significant increases in warfighter capability.

Research Opportunities

- Solid-State Fiber Laser Weapons
- Incoherent Fiber Laser
- Coherent Combined Fiber Laser
- Beam Control
- Modeling & Simulation
- Power Scaling

Solid-State Fiber Laser

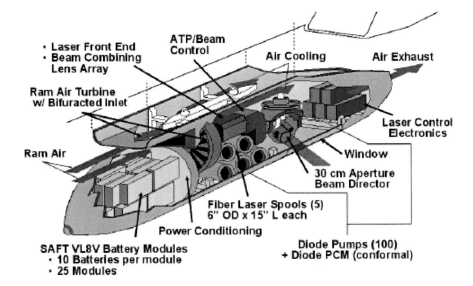

In: Navy Shipboard Lasers ISBN: 978-1-61324-212-4
Editors: R. E. Griffith, G. L. Coughlin © 2011 Nova Science Publishers, Inc.

Chapter 3

HIGH-POWER FIBER LASERS FOR DIRECTED-ENERGY APPLICATIONS

P. Sprangle, A. Ting, J. Peñano, R. Fischer and B. Hafizi

SUMMARY

High-power fiber lasers can be incoherently combined to form the basis of a high-energy laser system for directed-energy applications. These applications include tactical directed energy and power beaming. Incoherent combining of fiber lasers has a number of advantages over other laser beam combining methods. The incoherently combined laser system is relatively simple, highly efficient, compact, robust, low-maintenance, and reliable. In this article, we characterize the atmospheric propagation of incoherently combined, high optical quality laser beams and compare them with other types of laser beams and combining methods. For tactical directed-energy applications, we find that the propagation efficiency of incoherently combined high optical quality beams is near the theoretical upper limit for any laser system with the same beam director and total power. We present results of the first atmospheric propagation experiments using incoherently combined, kilowatt-class, single-mode fiber lasers. These NRL field experiments combined four fiber lasers using a beam director consisting of individually controlled steering mirrors. The transmitted continuous-wave power was 3 kW at a range of 1.2 km with a demonstrated propagation efficiency of ~90% in moderate atmospheric turbulence. The experimental results are found to be in good agreement with simulations and theory.

INTRODUCTION

The successful development of laser weapons promises to have a profound impact on military missions throughout the services. A directed-energy (DE) laser system must be capable of delivering hundreds of kilowatts of average power to a target at multi-kilometer ranges through adverse atmospheric conditions. In addition, the laser system must be efficient, compact, robust, and reliable. While a great deal of progress has been made toward this objective, the goal will soon receive a significant boost due to advances in high-power fiber laser technology. High-power fiber lasers can also have applications in the area of power beaming, e.g., to UAVs and low-orbit satellites.

To achieve the total laser power needed for tactical DE and power beaming applications it is necessary to combine a large number of fiber lasers. Lasers can be combined coherently, spectrally, or incoherently. This article focuses on incoherent combining of high-power, high optical quality fiber lasers. This laser beam combining approach has a number of advantages over coherent or spectral combining.

In this article we discuss the characteristics of high-power fiber lasers and the progress made in increasing the output power of these devices while maintaining high optical quality. In addition, we discuss and compare the propagation efficiency of incoherently combined fiber laser arrays and coherently combined arrays in realistic atmospheric conditions for multi-kilometer propagation ranges. We conclude by presenting results from the first field propagation experiments which demonstrate high-power, kilometer-range incoherent combining. In these NRL experiments, four single-mode fiber lasers capable of transmitting a combined continuous-wave (CW) power of 6.2 kW were incoherently combined on a target at a range of 1.2 km. The total volume occupied by the four fiber lasers, including power supply, diode pump lasers, and fibers, is less than 2 m^3. In the experiments, a total of 3 kW was transmitted over a 1.2 km range to a 10 cm radius target with the lasers at half power. Propagation efficiencies of ~90% were demonstrated in a moderately turbulent environment.

HIGH-POWER FIBER LASERS

Although a number of companies manufacture high-power fiber lasers, IPG Photonics Corp. (MA) currently has the most powerful, with over 3 kW per fiber of single-mode optical radiation.[1] Nufern (CT) now has a 1 kW, single-mode fiber laser available.[2] The term "single-mode" laser beam is synonymous with a diffraction-limited ideal Gaussian beam. The optical quality of a laser beam is measured in terms of the parameter M^2, which characterizes the laser beam spreading angle. An ideal Gaussian beam, i.e., single-mode beam, is characterized by an M^2 of unity and has the smallest spreading angle of any beam profile with the same spot size (radius). Multi-mode beams have an M^2 greater than unity. The diffraction (spreading) angle of multi-mode beams is M^2 times greater than that of a single-mode (ideal Gaussian) beam. For long-range propagation, single-mode beams are necessary.

Figure 1 illustrates the progress made in recent years in increasing the power in single-mode fiber lasers. It is anticipated that the power output of single-mode fiber lasers will reach a plateau of ~5 kW/fiber in approximately one year. Multi-kilowatt, single-mode fiber lasers are robust, compact, and have high wall-plug efficiency, random polarization, and large bandwidth (~0.1%). A 1 kW, single-mode IPG fiber laser module, operating at wavelength $\lambda = 1.075$ µm, excluding power supply, measures w × h × d ~ 60 cm × 33 cm × 5 cm, weighs approximately 20 lbs, has a wall-plug efficiency of >30%, and has an operating lifetime in excess of 10,000 hrs. Figure 2 shows a 1.2 kW fiber laser module manufactured by IPG. The total weight of a 2 kW IPG fiber laser, including power supply, is ~330 lbs. Because of the high operating efficiency, only a moderate degree of water cooling is required, i.e., ~2 gallons/ minute/kW. To operate in a single mode, the optical core radius of the fiber must be sufficiently small. For example, the IPG single-mode 1 kW fiber lasers have an optical core radius of ~15 µm. Multi-mode IPG fibers, on the other hand, operating at 10 kW (20 kW) per fiber have an optical core radius of ~100 µm (~200 µm) and $M^2 \sim 13$ ($M^2 \sim 38$). These higher-power fiber lasers with larger values of M^2 have a more limited propagation range.

FIBER LASER COMBINING

To achieve the power levels needed for DE applications it is necessary to combine a large number of fiber lasers either coherently, spectrally, or incoherently. Coherent and spectral combining of laser beams can, in principle, result in a smaller size beam director. Coherent combining seeks to construct a phase-locked optical wavefront from many individual lasers, thus increasing the effective laser spot size and extending the propagation range. However, this approach requires extremely narrow laser linewidths and precise control of the polarization and phase of the individual lasers. Fiber lasers with the narrow line widths required for coherent combining are currently limited in power to less than a few hundred watts per fiber due to inherent nonlinearities which broaden the linewidth. Spectral combining uses gratings to combine a large number of beams with slightly different wavelengths. This approach is also limited by the fiber laser bandwidth and the requirement that the lasers have a well-defined polarization. To date, the highest total power achieved through coherent or spectral combining is less than 1 kW. Using currently available fiber lasers, a coherently or spectrally combined DE system would be complex and require an extremely large number of lasers.

Incoherent combining has a number of advantages over coherent and spectral combining. This approach does not require narrow linewidths or phase/polarization locking of the individual lasers. Hence, it allows for the use of higher-power, multi-kilowatt fiber lasers and is much easier to implement. Incoherent combining of laser beams is achieved by overlapping the individual laser beams on a target with a beam director consisting of independently controlled steering mirrors and beam expanders[3] as shown in Fig. 3. To limit diffractive spreading over the propagation range, the spot size of the beams must be large enough at the source and the beams must have good optical quality. In the absence of turbulence, the effective range of an incoherently combined array of single-mode lasers is determined by the Rayleigh range (ZR) of an individual beam, which is given by $Z_R \sim R_o^2 / \lambda$, where Ro is the initial beam spot size and λ is the laser wavelength. To achieve efficient propagation, the distance to the target (target range), L, should be less than ~2ZR. For example, a single-mode fiber laser with initial spot size Ro = 4 cm and wavelength λ = 1 μm has a Rayleigh range of ~5 km, so the target range should be less than ~10 km to avoid significant diffractive spreading. Usually, however, the spreading of the beam is dominated by atmospheric turbulence and not diffraction. This situation is discussed in the next section.

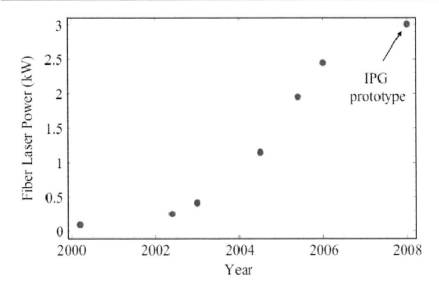

Figure 1. Progress made in increasing the power per fiber in single-mode fiber lasers.

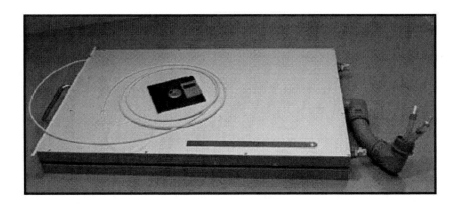

Figure 2. IPG Photonics 1.2 kW fiber laser module. Module has dimensions 60 x 33 x 5 cm, weight ~20 lbs, and wall-plug efficiency ~30%.

Because incoherent combining allows for a higher power per fiber, the laser system is compact and readily scalable to power levels needed for DE applications. For N incoherently combined fiber lasers, the total transmitted power is N times the power in the individual fiber, and the beam director radius is $R_{BD} \approx \sqrt{N} R_o$.

A 500 kW laser system would consist of 100 fiber lasers (5 kW/fiber), have a beam director radius of ~40 cm, and, excluding power supply, the fibers and pump diodes would occupy a volume of ~8 m^3.

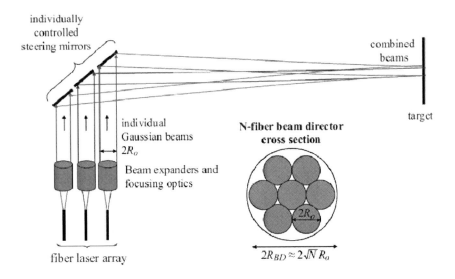

Figure 3. Schematic diagram of incoherently combined fiber laser beams directed to a target.

ATMOSPHERIC PROPAGATION OF LASER BEAMS

The physical processes affecting the propagation of high-power laser beams in the atmosphere are complex and interrelated. These processes include diffraction, molecular/aerosol scattering and absorption, turbulence produced by air density fluctuations, thermal blooming, and others. While it is beyond the scope of this article to consider these physical processes in detail, for the purpose of estimating and comparing the propagation efficiency of combined single-mode and multi-mode fiber lasers we consider some of the more important processes in a simplified manner. We also discuss the use of tip-tilt compensation in the beam director to correct for the wander of the laser beam centroid due to turbulence, and quantify its limitations.

The minimum laser beam spot size, or radius, is obtained by adjusting the focal length of the transmitted beam so it equals the distance to the target, or range L. The laser beam spot size on target is then given by R = $\Box_{spread}$ spread L

where the spreading angle θ_{spread} is the sum of contributions from diffraction, θ_{diff}, atmospheric turbulence, θ_{turb}, mechanical jitter, θ_{jitter}, and thermal blooming, θ_{bloom}. Thermal blooming, i.e., the self-defocusing of the laser due to absorption and the subsequent heating of the air, can be partially mitigated by propagating in an atmospheric transmission window where the absorption is low. Fortuitously the fiber laser wavelength, $\lambda = 1.075$ µm, is near a narrow water vapor transmission window centered at $\lambda = 1.045$ µm. In the presence of water-based aerosols the actual transmission window is broadened[4] and easily includes the fiber laser wavelength. For total laser power levels less than ~100 kW, and depending on the transverse air flow and atmospheric absorption, thermal blooming effects can usually be neglected.[3] Thermal blooming near the beam director can be eliminated by introducing a transverse air flow.[5] For the purposes of this discussion we will also neglect the small mechanical jitter contribution and concentrate on the dominant effects of turbulence and diffraction.

Atmospheric turbulence strength is described by the parameter C_n^2, which characterizes the amplitude of density fluctuations in the air. C_n^2 normally ranges from 10^{-15} m$^{-2/3}$ (weak turbulence) to 10^{-13} m$^{-2/3}$ (very strong turbulence). The effect of turbulence on laser beam propagation is characterized by the Fried parameter (transverse coherence length), r_o, which is a function of C_n^2 and propagation range. The Fried parameter varies from tens of centimeters for weak turbulence conditions to fractions of a centimeter for strong turbulence. The spreading angle of a laser beam due to atmospheric turbulence is $\theta_{turb} = 1.6 \lambda / \pi R_o$.[6,7]

Comparison of Single- and Multi-Mode Propagation

The diffractive spreading angle of an individual laser beam is $\theta_{diff} = M^2 \lambda/(\pi R_o)$. The goal of coherent combining is to reduce the diffractive spreading angle by phase locking and polarization locking N individual single-mode lasers, thus increasing the effective spot size by a factor of $\sqrt{N}$. For single-mode fiber lasers propagating over long distances, turbulence spreading dominates diffractive spreading, i.e., $\theta_{turb} \gg \theta_{diff}$, since the Fried parameter is usually less than the initial laser spot size, $r_o \ll R_o$. On the other hand, for highly multi-mode fibers ($M^2 \gg 1$), the diffractive spreading angle can be large, i.e., $\theta_{turb} > \theta_{diff}$. These differences between single-mode and multi-mode fibers have important consequences for their propagation efficiency and the use of adaptive optics to reduce the effects of turbulence. For single-mode fibers, the use of adaptive optics can substantially improve the propagation efficiency. However, for multi-mode fibers, adaptive optics will have little effect on the propagation efficiency because the main contribution to the spreading angle is from diffraction due to poor beam quality, i.e., high value of M^2.

To determine the merits of incoherently combining single-mode or multi-mode fiber lasers for DE applications, it is useful to compare their propagation efficiencies. Here, we define propagation efficiency as the ratio of power on target to total transmitted laser power. In making this comparison, the fiber laser systems are assumed to have the same size beam director and the same total power. Table 1 lists the parameters of four systems that are designed to deliver a total power of 100 kW. The systems are based on currently available fiber lasers. For example, for the 3 kW per fiber and $M^2 = 1$ case, 33 fiber lasers (N_{fiber}) are required to achieve 100 kW. The corresponding M^2 values reflect the fact that for multi-mode lasers the beam quality decreases (M^2 increases) as the power per fiber increases. Table 1 also gives the radius of the collimating lens for the individual fiber lasers (R_o). In all cases, the radius of the beam director is 50 cm and the target is assumed to be a circular disc with a surface area of 100 cm^2. Figure 4 plots the propagation efficiency for $M^2 = 1$, 7, and 38, in vacuum (Fig. 4(a)), and in a turbulent environment with $C_n^2 = 10^{-14}$m$^{-2/3}$ (Figs. 4(b) and (c)). In all cases, the beams are focused onto the target. For propagation through turbulence, Fig. 4 shows the efficiency without adaptive optics (b) and with adaptive optics (c). The adaptive optics was modeled, in the results shown in Fig. 4(c), by increasing the Fried parameter by a factor of four. The dashed curves denote the case of a single ideal Gaussian beam with initial spot size equal to the radius of the beam director, i.e., the theoretical upper limit for perfectly coherently combined beams. For ranges <10 km in vacuum (Fig. 4(a)), and for conditions in which turbulence dominates (Fig. 4(b)), the single-mode incoherently combined example (red curve) has a propagation efficiency virtually identical to that of the coherently combined beam (dashed curve), while the propagation efficiency of the various multi-mode fibers is far less. Figure 4 also shows that the use of adaptive optics can greatly improve the propagation efficiency of combined single-mode fibers but has little effect on the combined multi-mode fiber lasers.

Table 1. Four configurations of a 100 kW system using single-mode and multi-mode fiber lasers. Systems are labeled by color to match propagation efficiency plotted in Fig. 4. The black, dashed curve in Fig. 4 denotes an ideal Gaussian beam having a 50 cm spot size

Power/fiber (kW)	M^2	N_{fiber}	R_o(cm)
3	1	33	8.7
5	7	20	11.2
20	38	5	22.4
100	1	1	50

Comparison of Incoherent and Coherent Combining

It is often stated that the advantage of coherent beam combining is that, for a given size beam director and total power level, coherent combining results in a smaller beam spreading angle compared with incoherently combined beams. For propagation in vacuum, the brightness (intensity/solid angle) of the coherently combined fiber array is N times larger than for an incoherently combined array, where N is the number of fibers. While this is true for vacuum propagation, it is not relevant when the effects of atmospheric turbulence are taken into account. Beam brightness at the source is of limited importance when considering realistic DE propagation scenarios in turbulent atmospheres.

When the turbulence strength is large enough so that the Fried parameter, r_o, is less than the beam director radius, R_{BD}, coherent and incoherent combining give comparable values for spreading angle and spot size on target. This condition is usually satisfied for DE applications. For example, in moderate turbulence and a propagation distance of $L = 2$ km, the Fried parameter is $r_o = 3$ cm, which is typically much smaller than the beam director radius. As shown in Fig. 4(b), the power on target for an incoherently combined array of single-mode lasers with $N = 33$ (red curve) is virtually identical to that of a coherently combined array (dashed curve).

Compared to a coherently combined array, incoherently combined fiber lasers can deliver similar power levels to a remote target. This is seen by comparing the dashed (coherent array) and red (incoherent array) curves in Fig. 4(a). For typical propagation scenarios and realistic atmospheric conditions, there is little if any advantage to coherently combining laser beams as compared to incoherently combining them.

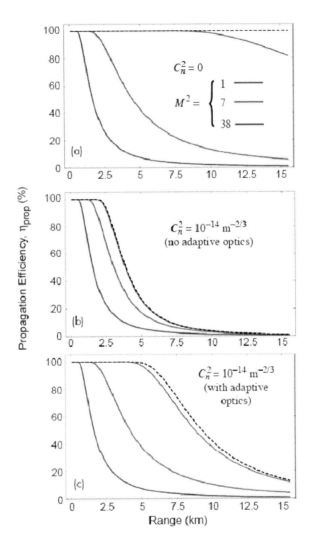

Figure 4. Propagation efficiency versus range for incoherently combined fiber laser beams with beam quality parameters $M^2 = 1$, 7, and 38: (a) in vacuum, (b) in a turbulent atmosphere with $C_n^2 = 10^{-14}$ m$^{-2/3}$ (no adaptive optics), and (c) in a turbulent atmosphere with adaptive optics. Laser parameters are listed in Table 1. The dashed curve represents the theoretical upper limit for coherent and incoherent combining.

Beam Wander and Tip-Tilt Compensation

Introducing tip-tilt correction into the individual steering mirrors can reduce the overall laser spot size on target. Tip-tilt correction redirects the centroids of the individual laser beams to cancel the effects of wander due to turbulence. This is accomplished by monitoring the intensity on target and redirecting the steering mirrors to minimize the spot size. Laser beam wander is a function of the scale size of the turbulence fluctuations. Turbulent eddies that are large compared to the laser beam diameter cause the laser beam centroid to be deflected and to wander in time due to transverse air flow. Eddies that are much smaller than the beam diameter cause spreading about the beam centroid and cannot be reduced by the use of tip-tilt compensation. The observed long time averaged laser spot size is a combination of beam wander and spreading about the centroid. In weak turbulence, the beam centroid wander represents a significant contribution to the laser beam radius. As the turbulence level increases, or for long propagation ranges, the beam wander contribution to the laser spot size becomes less important. In very strong turbulence, the laser beam breaks up into multiple beams making tip-tilt compensation ineffective.

If the individual laser beams are separated by less than r_o at the source, the wander of the centroids on the target will be correlated. In this case, it would be possible for beams to share a common tip-tilt correcting aperture, thus reducing the size and complexity of the system.

NRL FIBER LASER EXPERIMENTS

The NRL incoherent combining field propagation experiments use four IPG single-mode fiber lasers having a total output power of 6.2 kW (1 kW, 1.6 kW, 1.6 kW, and 2 kW). These initial experiments were performed at the Naval Surface Warfare Center (NSWC) in Dahlgren, VA, over a propagation range of 1.2 km. An aerial view of the propagation range is shown in Fig. 5. The laser beams propagated 4 to 10 ft above a blacktop road.

The beam director consists of four fiber output couplers and individually controlled steering mirrors which direct the four single-mode fiber laser beams onto a target. Each beam has a spot size of —2.5 cm as it exits the beam director and the target is a 10-cmradius, water-cooled power meter.

Figure 6 shows a schematic of the fiber laser output coupler and the beam expander (concave-convex lens combination) which is used to adjust the focal length. In these initial experiments the fiber lasers were operated at nearly half power because of thermal blooming in the beam director and in the atmosphere just beyond the laser source. These issues can be readily corrected in the next series of experiments by using lower-absorption optics and inducing air flow near the laser output. Thermal effects caused an axial shift of the focus with time as the total laser power was increased to —3 kW. The change in the focal length was compensated for by changing the separation between the lenses in the beam expander. Figure 7 shows the beam director, output couplers, and steering mirrors used in the experiments.

The power on target as a function of time is shown in Fig. 8. After the output coupler reached thermal equilibrium (> 200 sec), the measured power was 2.8 kW, corresponding to a propagation efficiency of ~ 90%. The typical errors associated with the measured transmitted power and power on target was ±5%.

Atmospheric turbulence causes the laser beams on target to wander and change shape. Since the laser beam separation is initially much greater than r_o, the individual beams are uncorrelated and their centroids randomly wander with respect to each other. At times, the four beams completely overlap forming a single spot, while at other times the four individual beams are separated by typically a few centimeters. The characteristic time scale associated with beam wander is ~ 20 msec. Since the mechanical jitter angle was measured to be less than ~ 2 μrad, the beam centroid wander is caused mainly by atmospheric turbulence.

Figure 9 displays two frames from a CCD camera, the first at ~ 180 sec and the second at ~ 300 sec, showing 2.8 kW of combined laser power on the power meter. The two frames were chosen to illustrate cases where the four beam centroids are fully overlapped and where they have maximum displacement from each other. Precise measurements of beam wander and spreading at the target are difficult and were not available for these preliminary experiments because of pixel saturation in the camera and a limited number of frame samples. However, one can estimate the beam wander and spot size from the CCD images. The lower panel of Fig. 9 indicates that the average centroid wander was ~ 4 cm and that the individual instantaneous laser spot size was ~ 2.5 cm. Hence, the long time average spot size is estimated to be R~ 4.7 cm.

To compare the experimental observations with simulations and theory, the atmospheric turbulence level, C_n^2, was measured using a scintillometer. The average value of C_n^2 during the experiments was ~ 5×10^{-14}m$^{-2/3}$ and the average transverse wind velocity was estimated to be ~ 2.5 m/sec.

Comparison of Experiments with Simulations and Theory

The Navy's High-Energy Laser Code for Atmospheric Propagation (HELCAP)[3,4,5] was used to model the propagation experiments. The HELCAP code is fully three-dimensional, time-dependent, and includes molecular/aerosol scattering/absorption, turbulence, and thermal blooming effects. The simulations assume an aerosol scattering coefficient of 0.05 km^{-1} and 1 μrad of mechanical jitter.[3]

Figure 5. Aerial view of the laser propagation range in Dahlgren, VA.

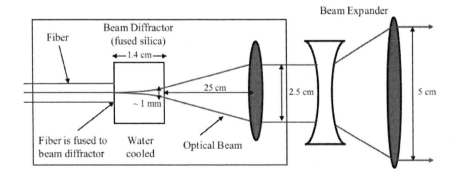

Figure 6. Schematic diagram of fiber output coupler and beam expander.

Figure 7. Beam director used for incoherent combining. Three of four fiber output couplers are shown in the foreground. Four individually controlled steering mirrors are shown in the background.

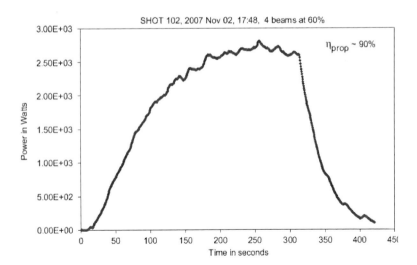

Figure 8. Experimentally measured power at target versus time. Target was a power meter with 45 sec response time and 10 cm radius. Average wind speed was ~2.5 m/sec, and measured turbulence strength $C_n = 5 \times 10^{-14} \, m^{-2/3}$. The maximum propagation efficiency is ~90%. Thermal equilibrium in the power meter is reached at ~200 sec and the laser beams are turned off at ~320 sec.

High-Power Fiber Lasers for Directed-Energy Applications   79

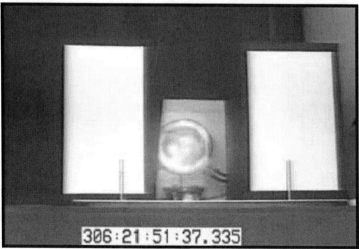

Figure 9. Two CCD camera images of four beams incoherently combined on target (10 cm radius power meter) at a range of 1.2 km. The first panel shows the combined beams at ~180 sec and the second image is at ~300 sec. The later image shows the four individual beam centroids randomly displaced by ~4 cm due to atmospheric turbulence.

Figure 10 shows the results of HELCAP simulations in which four laser beams, with a total power of 3 kW and at a range of 1.2 km, were incoherently combined. Panel (a) shows the intensity contours of the four beams at the fiber laser output coupler. The focal length of each beam was adjusted to minimize the spot size on target. Panel (b) shows time-averaged (over a few seconds) intensity contours of the combined laser beam on the target plane. The long time average spot size on target from the simulations was ~4.6 cm compared with the experimental estimate of 4.7 cm. The intensity profile as a function of time indicates that the rms wander displacement from the simulations was ~2.5 cm compared with the experimental estimate of 4 cm. The instantaneous spot size of the individual beams from the simulations was ~3.1 cm compared with the experimental estimate of 2.7 cm.

Using atmospheric turbulence theory[3,6,7] we calculated the laser beam wander displacement and long time averaged spot size. The calculated beam wander and long time average spot size was 2.8 cm and 4.2 cm, respectively. These calculated values are in good agreement with experimental observations and HELCAP simulations.

DISCUSSION

In 2008, the NRL fiber lasers will be moved to the Starfire Optical Range in Albuquerque, NM, and propagation experiments over a 3.2 km range will take place at full power. The objectives of these experiments are to demonstrate the incoherent beam combining concept at longer range, quantify thermal blooming effects, more precisely characterize the beam wander and spreading, and validate the propagation model (HELCAP). Planned experiments will incorporate target-in-the-loop tip-tilt compensation into one of the fiber laser beams to correct for wandering of the beam centroid. Controlled thermal blooming experiments can also be carried out using a stagnation tube to eliminate the cooling effects of transverse air flow. This arrangement permits thermal blooming effects to be observed under controlled conditions and at relatively low power levels. The temporal change in the laser spot size and intensity and measurements of the air properties inside the stagnation tube will provide the necessary data to study atmospheric thermal blooming under realistic conditions.

In addition to the NRL program, other fiber laser–based DE efforts are underway. A NAVSEA lethality/propagation program being carried out at NSWC Dahlgren utilizes six multi-mode fiber lasers, each having a CW power of 5 kW and optical quality of $M^2 \sim 6$. A joint Pennsylvania State University/NSWC Crane lethality and propagation program is also under way using two multi-mode fiber lasers, 10 kW ($M^2 \sim 13$) and 5 kW ($M^2 \sim 6$).

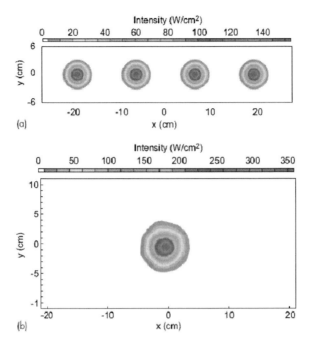

Figure 10. HELCAP simulation showing a time-averaged transverse intensity profile of laser beams at (a) the source and (b) incoherently combined on target at a range of 1.2 km. The atmospheric turbulence level used in the simulation is the same as those measured in the experiment.

SUMMARY

Incoherent combining of high-power fiber lasers can result in highly efficient, compact, robust, low-maintenance, and long-lifetime high-energy laser systems for directed-energy applications. In this article, we discussed the propagation of incoherently combined single-mode and multi-mode fiber laser beams through atmospheric turbulence. We compared the propagation efficiency of coherent and incoherent combining and found that under typical atmospheric conditions and propagation ranges, the propagation efficiency of incoherently combined single-mode fiber lasers is nearly identical to the theoretical upper limit for coherent combining. Hence, there is no inherent advantage to coherently combining beams for tactical directed-energy scenarios.

We presented results from the first field demonstration experiments of long-range incoherent combining. The experiments combined four fiber lasers using a beam director consisting of individually controlled steering mirrors. Propagation efficiencies of ~90%, at a range of 1.2 km, with transmitted CW power levels of 3 kW were demonstrated in moderate turbulence. Numerical simulations and theoretical results were in good agreement with experimental observation.

The NRL propagation experiments have provided important information concerning the issues associated with incoherently combining high-power, single-mode fiber lasers. These field experiments will lay the groundwork for developing a tactical DE laser system in the near term.

ACKNOWLEDGMENTS

We acknowledge C. Rollins, G. Dicomo, Z. Wilkes, and J. Caron for their assistance in the field experiments.

[Sponsored by NRL, ONR, and HEL-JTO]

End Notes

[1] V. Gapontsev et al., "2 kW CW Ytterbium Fiber Laser with Record Diffraction-Limited Brightness," in *2005 Conference on Lasers and Electro-Optics Europe (CLEO Europe)*, p. 508 (2005).

[2] J. Edgecumbe, "Kilowatt Level, Monolithic Fiber Amplifiers for Beam Combining Applications at 1 µm," *Proceedings of the 20th Solid State and Diode Laser Technology Review* (2007).

[3] P. Sprangle, J. Peñano, B. Hafizi, and A. Ting, "Incoherent Combining of High-Power Fiber Lasers for Long-Range Directed Energy Applications," *Journal of Directed Energy* 2, 273-284 (2007); also NRL Memorandum Report, NRL/MR/6790-- 06-8963, June 2006.

[4] P. Sprangle, J. Peñano, and B. Hafizi, "Optimum Wavelength and Power for Efficient Laser Propagation in Various Atmospheric Environments," *Journal of Directed Energy* 2, 71-95 (2006).

[5] J.R. Peñano, P. Sprangle, and B. Hafizi, "Propagation of High Energy Laser Beams Through Atmospheric Stagnation Zones," *Journal of Directed Energy* 2, 107 (2006).

[6] L.C. Andrews and R.L. Phillips, *Laser Beam Propagation through Random Media*, 2nd ed. (SPIE Press, Bellingham, WA, 2005).

[7] R.L. Fante, "Electromagnetic Beam Propagation in Turbulent Media," *Proc. IEEE* 63, 1669-1692 (1975).

THE AUTHORS

PHILLIP SPRANGLE is chief scientist and head of the Beam Physics Branch of the Plasma Physics Division at NRL. He received a Ph.D. in physics from Cornell University in 1973. Dr. Sprangle's primary areas of research include high-energy and high-intensity laser physics, free-electron lasers, nonlinear optics, and laser plasma accelerators. Dr. Sprangle is the recipient of the 1986 E. O. Hulburt Science Award, the 1991 International Free Electron Laser Prize, the 1994 Sigma Xi Pure Science Award, and the IEEE Plasma Science and Applications Award. Dr. Sprangle is a Fellow of the American Physical Society, IEEE, and the Directed Energy Professional Society, and a member of Sigma Xi.

ANTONIO TING is head of the Laser Physics Section and a senior research physicist in the Beam Physics Branch of the Plasma Physics Division at NRL, where he has worked since 1988. His research areas include ultra-high-field physics, advanced particle accelerators, advanced radiation sources, and intense laser interactions with air, plasmas, and electron beams. Dr. Ting has published 101 refereed journal articles and holds three U.S. patents. He has presented 23 invited and review talks at professional and international conferences. He is a Fellow of the American Physical Society and member of Sigma Xi. He has twice won the NRL Alan Berman Publication Award and the 2003 *NRL Review* Award.

JOSEPH PEÑANO is head of the Radiation and Acceleration Physics Section of the Plasma Physics Division at NRL. He received a Ph.D. in physics from the University of California, Los Angeles, in 1998 and joined the NRL Plasma Physics Division in 2002. His research areas include high-energy and high-intensity laser physics; atmospheric propagation of high-energy and ultra-short-pulse lasers, interactions of intense ultra-short lasers with dielectric materials, detection of special nuclear materials, free-electron lasers, and laser plasma accelerators. Dr. Peñano holds two U.S. patents and is a winner of the 2002 NRL Alan Berman Publication Award, the 2003 Directed Energy Professional Society Best Paper Award, the *NRL Review* Featured Research Award in 2003, 2004, and 2008, and the 2003 NRL Technology Transfer Award.

RICHARD FISCHER received his B.S., M.S., and Ph.D. degrees in electrical engineering from the University of Maryland, College Park, in 1984, 1986, and 1993, respectively. He has been a researcher in the Plasma Physics Division at NRL since 1988. His recent research has concentrated on atmospheric laser propagation and the interaction of intense lasers with electron beams, semiconductors, and plasmas. This includes experiments on high-power fiber laser propagation, relativistic Thomson backscattering, athermal annealing of semiconductors, and the development of gyrotrons, quasi-optical gyrotrons, and quasioptical gyroklystrons. Dr. Fischer is a member of the American Physical Society.

BAHMAN HAFIZI received B.Sc. and Ph.D. degrees in physics from Imperial College, London, in 1974 and 1978. He is president of Icarus Research, Inc., and a theoretical research scientist at NRL. He previously worked as a research associate in the Department of Astro-Geophysics at the

University of Colorado and as a staff scientist for Science Applications International Corporation. His current research areas include propagation of ultra-intense laser pulses, laser-driven electron accelerators, free-electron lasers, laser-plasma interactions, and nonlinear optics. He has also worked on advanced sources of electromagnetic radiation and ultra-broadband sources, with application to imaging, lithography, and remote sensing. He is an Associate of the Royal College of Science and a member of the American Physical Society, the European Physical Society, and the IEEE.

In: Navy Shipboard Lasers ISBN: 978-1-61324-212-4
Editors: R. E. Griffith, G. L. Coughlin © 2011 Nova Science Publishers, Inc.

Chapter 4

CCW: Article by Article Analysis of the Protocol on Blinding Laser Weapons

Article-by-Article Analysis of the Protocol on Blinding Laser Weapons Annexed to the Convention on Prohibitions or Restrictions on the Use of Certain Conventional Weapons which May Be Deemed to Be Excessively Injurious or to Have Indiscriminate Effects

(Protocol IV)

The Protocol on Blinding Laser Weapons (Protocol IV) is annexed to the Convention on Prohibitions or Restriction on the Use of Certain Conventional Weapons Which May be Deemed to be Excessively Injurious or to Have Indiscriminate Effects (the Convention).

The Convention, including three annexed protocols, was concluded at Geneva on October 10, 1980. The United States ratified the Convention and expressed its consent to be bound by its Protocol II on Mines, Booby-traps and Other Devices, as well as its Protocol I on Non-Detectable Fragments, on March 24, 1995.

In 1994, an international review of the Convention was begun to address, particular, the strenthening of the Mines Protocol. It also took under consideration the question of adopting a new protocol on blinding laser weapons. This international review process concluded in May of 1996 with the adoption of an amended Mines Protocol and a new Protocol IV on Blinding Laser Weapons. The provisions of the new Protocol are discussed, article by article, below.

The Blinding Laser Weapons Protocol consists of four articles.

Article 1

Article 1 prohibits the employment of "laser weapons specifically designed, as their sole combat function or as one of their combat functions, to cause permanent blindness to unenhanced vision, that is to the naked eye or to the eye with corrective eyesight devices." Article 1 also prohibits the transfer of any such weapon to any state or non-state entity.

This prohibition is fully consistent with the policy of the Department of Defense, which is to prohibit the use of weapons so designed. Although the prospect of mass blinding was an impetus for the adoption of the Protocol, it was not the intent of the Conference to prohibit only mass blinding. Accordingly, under both the Blinding Laser Protocol and Department of Defense policy, laser weapons designed specifically to cause such permanent blindness may not be used against an individual enemy combatant.

Article 2

Article 2 concerns lasers other than those described in Article 1 and obligates High Contracting Parties to "take all feasible precautions to avoid the incidence of permanent blindness to unenhanced vision."

This requirement is also fully consistent with the policy of the Department of Defense which is to reduce, through training and doctrine, inadvertent injuries from the use of lasers designed for other purposes, such as range-finding, target discrimination, and communications.

Article 3

Article 3 provides that "blinding as an incidental or collateral effect of the legitimate military employment of laser systems, including laser systems used against optical equipment, is not covered" by the Protocol.

Article 3 reflects a recognition of the inevitability of eye injury as the result of lawful battlefield laser use. Its use is an important measure in avoiding war crimes allegations where injury occurs from legitimate laser uses.

Article 4

Article 4 defines permanent blindness as "irreversible and uncorrectable loss of vision which is seriously disabling with no prospect of recovery. Serious disability is equivalent to visual acuity of less than 20/200 Snellen measured in both eyes."

This definition of the term "permanent blindness" is of sufficient precision to prevent misuse or misunderstanding of the term which is a critical element of Article 1. It is also consistent with widely accepted ophthalmological standards.

Entry into Force

The entry into force provision refers to the procedures contained in the main Convention. Those procedures provide that the new protocols, such as the Blinding Laser Weapons Protocol, will enter into force six months after twenty states have notified their consent to be bound.

Scope of Application of the Protocol

The Protocol contains no provision regarding its scope of application. The Convention itself extends only to international armed conflicts (and to internal conflicts for "national liberation"). At the time of drafting and adoption of the Protocol participants were aware that it was proposed to extend the scope of the Mines Protocol to internal conflicts. However, at the final session of the CCW Review conference, certain states were unwilling to extend the scope of the Blinding Laser Weapons Protocol, despite having done so for the Mines Protocol. As a result, the scope of the Blinding Laser Weapons Protocol is limited to the scope of the CCW.

The United States favored an expanded scope of application for the Blinding Laser Weapons Protocol. As a matter of policy, the United States will refrain from the use of laser weapons prohibited by the Protocol. Therefore, while the Blinding Laser Weapons Protocol does not legally apply to all armed conflicts, it is U.S. policy to apply the Protocol to all such conflicts, however they may be characterized, and in peacetime.

SUMMARY

The Protocol is fully consistent with U.S. military interests, Department of Defense policy and humanitarian concerns generally. Accordingly, the United States should ratify it at an early date.

(The above Treaty Compliance on Blinding Laser Weapons was taken from http://www.dod.gov/acq/acic/treaties/ccwapl/artbyart_pro4.htm on Feb. 7, 2011)

CHAPTER SOURCES

Chapter 1 - This is an edited, reformatted and augmented version of a Congressional Research Service publication, R41526, dated January 14, 2011

Chapter 2 - This is an edited, reformatted and augmented version of a U.S. Office of Naval Research publication, dated August, 2008.

Chapter 3 - This is an edited, reformatted and augmented version of a U.S. Office of Naval Research publication, ITS-02, dated August, 2008.

Chapter 4 - This is an edited, reformatted and augmented version of a U.S. Department of Defense Treaty Compliance publication, dated February 7, 2011.

INDEX

A

accelerator, 41, 43, 44, 57
advancements, 19
aerosols, 71
Afghanistan, 21
Air Force, 13, 35, 50, 51, 54, 55
amplitude, 71
annealing, 85
appropriations, 35
armed conflict, 47, 89, 90
assault, 25, 26, 27, 57
assessment, 51
assets, 32
atmosphere, 7, 15, 70, 74, 76
atoms, 57
attacker, 5, 57
avoidance, 49
awareness, 20

B

backscattering, 85
ballistic missiles, vii, 1, 3, 9, 10, 11, 16, 24, 31, 32, 53
bandwidth, 67, 68
base, 4
beams, viii, 34, 38, 65, 67, 68, 70, 72, 73, 74, 75, 76, 78, 79, 80, 81, 84, 85
benefits, 20, 48, 49, 58
blindness, 46, 47, 48, 58, 59, 88, 89

C

challenges, 7, 14, 15, 20, 21
chemicals, 54
Chief of Staff, 52
China, vii, 1, 3, 10, 12, 33, 38, 52, 58
classification, 50
climate, 17
climate change, 17
coherence, 71
collateral, 6, 9, 47, 48, 49, 53, 58, 62, 89
collateral damage, 6, 9, 48, 49, 53, 58, 62
commercial, 16, 23, 34, 57
communication, 62
communities, 20
community, 18, 19, 20, 21, 45, 49, 50
compensation, 70, 75, 80
competition, 22
competitors, 23
complexity, 23, 24, 54, 75
composition, 41
computing, 17
conference, 89
conflict, 9
Congressional Budget Office, 4
consent, viii, 87, 89
construction, 24
containers, 53, 56
convention, 46

cooling, 6, 9, 14, 25, 26, 28, 34, 38, 67, 80
cost, 2, 3, 5, 7, 9, 12, 18, 19, 21, 22, 23, 24, 27, 28, 29, 53, 54
CRS report, 53
cruise missiles, 5, 32
crystalline, 33, 38

D

danger, 21
density fluctuations, 70, 71
Department of Defense, vii, 1, 3, 28, 47, 58, 59, 88, 90
Department of Energy, 41
destruction, 48, 58
detection, 14, 48, 55, 58, 84
diffraction, 53, 67, 68, 70, 71, 72
diodes, 34, 70
disability, 89
discrimination, 47, 55, 88
displacement, 76, 80
dominance, 17
drawing, 25
dysprosium, 61

E

electricity, 5, 6, 33
electromagnetic, 8, 57, 86
electron, 1, 11, 20, 41, 43, 44, 83, 84, 85, 86
electrons, 41, 44, 57
employment, 20, 46, 47, 49, 56, 88, 89
energy, vii, 1, 3, 4, 14, 15, 16, 17, 20, 21, 25, 34, 38, 41, 42, 48, 49, 52, 54, 56, 57, 58, 65, 66, 81, 83, 84
energy recovery, 41
engineering, 14, 15, 22, 51, 85
environment, 12, 13, 14, 15, 17, 23, 46, 56, 66, 72
equilibrium, 76, 78
equipment, 24, 26, 41, 47, 89
Europe, 82
exploitation, 45
exposure, 49

F

feasability, 28
fiber, vii, 1, 11, 12, 15, 21, 23, 25, 33, 34, 38, 57, 61, 62, 65, 66, 67, 68, 69, 70, 71, 72, 73, 74, 75, 77, 78, 79, 80, 81, 82, 85
fibers, 33, 38, 61, 66, 67, 70, 71, 72, 73
fidelity, 28, 29
fire suppression, 54
fires, 6, 54
flexibility, 19
fluctuations, 75
force, 20, 21, 30, 48, 50, 51, 52, 56, 89
Ford, 26, 27, 57
funding, 2, 4, 13, 21, 26, 27, 29, 34, 35, 38, 42, 50, 56

G

gratings, 68

H

Hezbollah, 9
history, 19, 21, 35
human, 22, 23, 24
humidity, 15, 23

I

ideal, 67, 72, 73
identification, 50
illumination, 58
image, 79
images, 43, 76, 79
improvements, 34
incidence, 47, 88
industrial environments, 23
industry, 4, 10, 11, 30, 32
inevitability, 47, 89
injuries, 47, 48, 58, 88
institutions, 21, 41
integration, 34
international law, 48
investment, 20

investments, 45
Iran, 9
Iraq, 21
isolation, 56
issues, 2, 4, 15, 17, 24, 76, 82

J

justification, 53

K

kill, 5, 53
knots, 54

L

laws, 48, 53
lead, 3, 18, 21, 34, 52
leadership, 45
lens, 72, 75
liberation, 89
life cycle, 29
lifetime, 67, 81
light, 6, 7, 9, 10, 17, 18, 22, 23, 24, 33, 34, 38, 41, 43, 44, 53, 54, 56, 57, 62
light beam, 10, 34
light-emitting diodes, 33
lithography, 86
logistics, 54
low temperatures, 41

M

magnetic field, 41
man, 15, 32, 55
management, 14, 15, 17, 22, 23, 24
manufacturing, 11, 51
Marine Corps, 13, 45
marine environment, 7, 13, 22
Maryland, 58, 85
mass, 45, 47, 88
materials, 12, 34, 84
matter, iv, 47, 90
measurements, 76, 80
media, 57
meter, 16, 75, 76, 78, 79

Mexico, 58
military, vii, 1, 2, 3, 4, 12, 13, 14, 17, 19, 20, 21, 28, 38, 47, 48, 49, 52, 54, 56, 58, 66, 89, 90
mission, 46, 49, 54, 55
missions, 21, 28, 29, 62, 66
misunderstanding, 89
misuse, 89
MLD, 2, 12, 13, 14, 19, 23, 24, 38, 39, 40, 52
models, 9

N

national security, 49
neglect, 71
neodymium, 33, 61
nonlinear optics, 83, 86

O

obstacles, 21
officials, 3, 49, 52
operations, 6, 8, 9, 11, 13, 15, 16, 20, 23, 29, 31, 32, 35, 46, 49, 53, 54, 55
optical fiber, 61
orbit, 66
overlap, 76
ownership, 51

P

Pacific, 33, 58
participants, 89
patents, 84
permit, 5, 6, 7, 11, 19, 22, 23, 49
Persian Gulf, 9
photons, 41, 57
physics, 62, 83, 84, 85
platform, 28, 29
PMS, 33, 57
polarization, 67, 68, 71
policy, 17, 46, 47, 48, 49, 58, 88, 90
policy makers, 49
policymakers, 12, 22
pollution, 7
praseodymium, 61

preparation, iv, 4
president, 85
principles, 45, 54, 55
project, 2, 12
propagation, viii, 61, 65, 66, 67, 68, 70, 71, 72, 73, 75, 76, 77, 78, 80, 81, 82, 84, 85, 86
protection, vii, 61, 62
prototype, 1, 3, 11, 12, 14, 16, 34, 36, 45, 46, 55
prototypes, 2, 3, 16

R

radar, 6, 9, 11, 54, 56
radiation, 67, 84, 86
Radiation, 84
radio, 44
radius, 66, 67, 69, 70, 72, 73, 75, 78, 79
recognition, 47, 89
recommendations, iv
recovery, 89
Reform, 52
rejection, 18
reliability, 22
remote sensing, 86
repair, 56
requirements, 4, 16, 17, 18, 41, 45, 49, 56
resistance, 18, 21
resources, 22, 56
response, 8, 17, 52, 78
response time, 78
risk, 6, 9, 17, 19, 45, 49, 54
risks, 13
rules, 49

S

safety, 49
saturation, 8, 53, 76
scaling, 12, 13, 14, 41
scatter, 7
scattering, 7, 10, 53, 54, 70, 77
science, 15, 42
scope, 45, 70, 89, 90

Secretary of Defense, 28, 29, 48, 50, 56, 58, 59
semiconductors, 85
seminars, 20
Senate, 28, 29
sensing, 55
sensors, 7, 9, 11, 12, 14, 15, 16
shape, 76
shock, 24
showing, 43, 76, 81
simulation, 62, 81
simulations, viii, 66, 76, 77, 79, 80, 82
socialization, 15, 18, 19, 55
software, 49
solid state, 1, 11, 28, 29, 33, 62
solution, 7, 22
specific surface, 2, 3, 4, 16, 17, 18, 27
specifications, 16
state, 9, 17, 20, 28, 88
states, 3, 12, 13, 14, 15, 16, 21, 28, 29, 43, 47, 49, 55, 57, 58, 89
stress, 6
submarines, 4
surface area, 72
susceptibility, 8, 10

T

tactics, 3
tanks, 56
target, 3, 5, 6, 7, 8, 9, 10, 13, 14, 34, 47, 48, 53, 54, 55, 58, 66, 68, 70, 72, 73, 75, 76, 78, 79, 80, 81, 88
technologies, vii, 2, 3, 16, 18, 19, 21, 45, 52, 56
technology, 11, 15, 17, 18, 19, 20, 22, 34, 45, 50, 55, 56, 62, 66
temperature, 41
terrorists, 21
testing, 16, 62
thermal energy, 34, 38, 41
threats, 4, 17, 32, 62
thulium, 61
time frame, 16
training, 47, 49, 58, 88
transformation, 17

transmission, 13, 22, 23, 24, 34, 38, 41, 71
treaties, 58, 59, 90
turbulence, viii, 7, 10, 54, 65, 68, 70, 71, 72, 73, 75, 76, 77, 78, 79, 80, 81, 82

U

U.S. policy, 47, 90
underwater vehicles, 17
uniform, 28, 29
unit cost, 29
United, viii, 46, 47, 48, 87, 90
United States, viii, 46, 47, 48, 87, 90
universities, 41

V

vacuum, 54, 72, 73, 74
validation, 12, 13, 14, 46
vapor, 7
vehicles, 13, 17, 50, 51, 52, 57
velocity, 76
vibration, 10, 24
vision, 2, 3, 15, 16, 47, 48, 52, 88, 89
visual acuity, 89

W

war, 47, 89
war crimes, 47, 89
Washington, 56, 59
waste, 6, 14, 24, 34, 38, 41, 56
waste heat, 6, 14, 24
water, 7, 12, 13, 32, 53, 67, 71, 75
water vapor, 7, 32, 53, 71
wave power, viii, 65
wavelengths, 8, 22, 23, 24, 53, 68
weapons, 2, 3, 4, 5, 6, 8, 9, 14, 15, 16, 17, 20, 21, 22, 25, 27, 46, 47, 48, 49, 54, 55, 56, 58, 66, 88, 90
weapons of mass destruction, 55
web, 44
welding, 11, 34, 57
Wisconsin, 58

Y

Yale University, 58
yield, 21
ytterbium, 61
yttrium, 33